"In a world where money oft̶ ̶ ̶ ̶ ̶ ̶ ̶ ̶ ̶ ̶ ̶ ̶ existence, Christopher Cervantes presents to us an experience-based, detailed acumen for financial growth and even fulfillment. And he does not end there. He continues on towards finding the TRUE meaning of life beyond personal material wealth. This book is for all of us who look for concrete ways to attain real financial independence and more . . ."

Rev. Fr. Mario Jose C. Ladra
Best Selling Author of
"Straight From The Heart . . . A Prayer Companion"

"A book for all—especially for YOUNG PROFESSIONALS. This will guide them on how to build and plan for their future at an early age."

Ms. Ruth Abayon
Editor and Ret. Teacher

This book will introduce you to understand financial planning. It defines the why, how you can make a strong foundation in the science and art of financial planning in the life of an individual. This is a must for all who wish to have financial freedom in any stage of their life.

Enrico Capule
Sr. Agency Manager
Capule Associates
Philam Life

Chris has always strived to "walk the talk" and this book tells what the "talk" is. I know that it is his heart's desire that the reader would then "walk" because he has been there, done that. A simple, understandable, but very powerful book.

Ms. Carol Regilme-Millan, CIS
Unit Manager • Millan Unit
Philam Life

Mr. Christopher Cervantes has been a Kuya to us. He is not just a financial planner but a friend who would support your aspirations, back up your decisions, widen your knowledge and gently motivate you to start the best life you deserve.

We are grateful that he was present at the beginning of building our own family for we started it right and we know we will go smoothly up until we retire. Love is not just the only reason for keeping a tight relationship as a couple. Being financially stable and always dreaming the best for your family will surely make your bond last forever. Kuya Chris will present you the best options and will constantly follow your steps towards financial freedom.

**Engr. Jose Enrico Lalangan and
Engr. Pearly Corotan-Lalangan**
Clients

The first time I met Christopher Cervantes I saw a humble person not making too much noise.

Soon, however, I realized that here I had a very smart and creative person in disguise. Nothing, not even the most drastic occurrences, could make him lose track. Always focused and solving uprising problems, before looking for the reason and learn from this. Discussing different items, stretching from work related issues to every day domestic problems, I found a very good sharp analyzer.

Soon enough I had to promote him to get maximum output onboard.

During his years as Chief Officer, he not only did his work very well, but soon also started night classes with the crew. This way, encouraging people, to educate themselves for better suitable positions and a more meaningful life.

When lecturing the crew, Chris soon found out that, seamen in general, have a very poor knowledge of how to take care of their income (too many "One day millionaires").

Chris took up Economical Studies back home and I understood he felt he had a mission

By the knowledge of Christopher's capacity, I surely can recommend this book created by him.

Capt. Rein Eduard Kagi
(Swedish National)
Master Mariner and
expert in Logistics
OSM Ship ManagementAB,
Gothenburg, Sweden.

FINANCIAL PLANNING FOR THE FAST CHANGING WORLD

How To Make Your Money And Yourself Grow At The Same Rate Than You Ever Dreamed Possible

By
Christopher G. Cervantes, RFP, CIS

PARTRIDGE
A Penguin Random House Company

To order additional copies of this book, contact
Toll Free 800 101 2657 (Singapore)
Toll Free 1 800 81 7340 (Malaysia)
orders.singapore@partridgepublishing.com

www.partridgepublishing.com/singapore

DEDICATION

This book is dedicated to God's gift to my
life—Matheuz, my son, to my new angel
Czaryn Alisa and to the woman who
brought them into this world—Malou.
To my mother—Dionever, who taught
me what unconditional love means.

I LOVE YOU ALL

And to all my clients who ask
for more, this is for you.

ACKNOWLEDGEMENTS

Virpi Hameen-Anttila, a Finnish writer once said *"Writing wasn't easy to start. After I finally did it, I realized it was the most direct contact possible with the part of myself I thought I had lost, and which I constantly find new things from. Writing also includes the possibility of living many lives as well as living in any time or world possible. I can satisfy my enthusiasm for research, but jump like a calf outside the strict boundaries of science. I can speak about things that are important to me and somebody listens. It's wonderful!"* This book, just like everything else I have created in my life, is not a product of my own effort and talents alone. I must acknowledge many of those who have encouraged and helped me in this adventure.

My deepest thanks to the crew and officers of MT Commencement, where this book was conceived. When I was just starting my talks about Financial Planning and personal growth development, you guys were my first audience, patient and forgiving. In spite of my being a novice in the field that I was talking about, you were able to admire and believe in what I said. I am also grateful to many friends, many seamen and OFWs, students, colleagues and clients who attended my seminars and who tested this material and have given feedback and encouragement.

I am eternally grateful to Carol Millan and Family. The Law of Attraction really works, when I was just dreaming about writing this book, the Universe found a way for me to have a good friend and sister like you. To her husband Pablo Millan, Jr. who untiringly shared the burdens of accuracy and coordination in the preparation of this work and to Jared Carl Millan for his great talent as editor and the artistic contributions of Jael Carlos Millan.

A million thanks to Ruth Abayon for the support and patience and encouragement you have shown me during the first editing—thank you. When I almost wanted to back out, her words gave me the courage to continue—you're a very special friend.

To my beloved wife—Malou, without her help, I would not have had the peace of mind and mental fortitude to write this book. I thank her for her love, understanding and friendship. To my three-year old son, Matheuz, who smiles at me that means he was delighted that I am done with my laptop because he can now use it to play Angry Birds.

I have been blessed with countless mentors. To Bro. Bo Sanchez, I have learned a lot from you through your newsletters and seminars—thank you for being an inspiration to many. To the RFP Institute family, thanks for all the technical knowledge I learned from you that I was able to apply for myself and later I was able to share to others. To my Philam Life family especially to my Unit Manager, Diony Evangelista and my Agency Manager, Enrico Capule. I offer my ceaseless thanks for allowing me to join your Associates and for your continuing support and tutelage.

And finally to the "Coffee Club" members; Carol Millan, Beth Tuanquin, Mabel de la Cruz, and Pat Garzon. Thanks for all the guidance and information of the intricate details of our "world".

TABLE OF CONTENTS

INTRODUCTION

We are living in an era of the fastest changes the world has ever known. This may yet be the greatest time in all of human history. Our ancestors just bothered themselves with finding shelter and a haven from the dangers that wild animals brought. Today we are terrified that someone's misguided finger will push the wrong button and obliterate the whole of humanity. Such has change and information technology brought us.

Before, our ancestors worried only about the food that they will eat for the day, and when the location they were living in could not provide it anymore, it was solved by just taking a few steps and those problems would be gone. Today, more and more people are becoming wealthy, not only with food, but also with all of the things that a human being can ever imagine. Before, somebody's wealth was measured by how much grain, cattle, or other commodities he had that he can barter for other things he wanted. Now, it's not only gold but how much money and how fat his bank account is that will determine his wealth.

We are amazed on how fast the list of Fortune 500 magazine's "Richest Man in the World" changes every year. We are even surprised by how rapidly the list of people who have become self-made millionaires grows each year. We are fortunate to witness this type of rapid wealth creation and transfer in all of human history.

And most amazing of all is that a vast majority of them started with nothing. You will hear story after story of financially successful personalities today and how they started from being broke or even from being a beggar at one point in their lives.

I grew up in one of the slum areas in Novaliches, Quezon City. Way back then we did not even have electricity. My mother and I lived together with my other relatives in a small house made out of scrap material. At night, when it was time to go to sleep we just laid our mat on the floor wherever we pleased. I didn't even know what a room was at that time. But as a kid it did not seem to be a problem for me, for all I cared about at that time was just to play, enjoy, and have a good time with the other kids in our area. Poverty was not in my vocabulary yet at that time. What it meant, and its significance, went way over my young mind.

Everything seemed to be perfect until the time I went to school and attended grade one. This was the first time I heard and understood the word poor, for whenever my classmate asked me where I lived and I told them where it was, they called me poor because I lived in a squatters' area. That moment, the word squatters' area was added to my vocabulary and it was the first time I finally understood the meaning of it.

Slowly, I came to understand the meaning of being poor and rich, and that we were not rich but poor. Though we know that rich and poor are not exact words and that it's relative, the meaning of it may be different for each one of us. I remember that we had a neighbor just a few houses away from us, meaning they too were squatters but I called them rich because they had a television set. During that time owning a television was a big deal. One time when I was watching TV through their window, their son who was a bit older than me closed the window to drive me out. With that experience I promised myself that one day I will be rich too and the first thing I will buy is a television set. And true enough, on my very first job, the first piece of property I bought was a television set.

As I grew up, the question of why I was born poor while my classmates were rich nagged me frequently, but as I became older I came to understand that my classmates and I were not so different at all. And as I searched for ways to become rich, the very word itself became complicated.

My mother said, "For you to become rich you must have a good education so you can have a good and secure job". The father of my classmate said, "No, you have to go to Saudi and work there, then you'll be rich".

Financial freedom, financial literacy—words that are fast becoming popular with today's breed of Filipinos, only boils down to an old notion—"I want to be rich!" But the question is, "How does one become rich?" It's a long journey for most people searching for the secret path to richness and only very few are able to find that road.

I was born to a very poor family in Bulan, Sorsogon in Bicol. My mother worked as a maid for one of the rich families in Naga City. Being the eldest in a family of 11 siblings, my Mom was forced to work as maid because her father died unexpectedly when she was still in her teen years. During her stay with the family where she was serving, the son of her employer became interested in her and BOOM I came out into this world. When the parents of my father (which I've never even met ever since] found out, they got furious and drove my mother out of their house. My mom had no choice but to raise me up alone.

She went back to her home town in Sorsogon and waited for me to be born. She admitted to me that there was point in her life when she contemplated putting me up for adoption, for fear of not being able to raise me on my own. But when she saw me for the first time, she immediately changed her mind.

She applied as a maid again in Tabaco, Albay. Even with a meager salary, she accepted the job but with the agreement that she could bring me with her. So while she was serving as maid, she was also taking care of me. When I was 6, a visiting family became interested in her and asked her if she wanted to go to Manila to serve them. My Mom agreed but again with the same condition that she will bring me too. Once more we became servants of a family living in Sta. Mesa. There, our lives became a bit more harsh, especially for my mom as she was always being nagged by her employer. She decided to flee from that place and we took shelter with my grandmother. We lived with her together with some other relatives in a small squatters' house in Novaliches.

But this book is not about my life story though I know that if I ever send my life story to any of these "teleseryes", I would surely win a time slot in their TV anthology programs. This book is about how I became financially free from the state of being so poor to having what I wanted in life and serving others to fulfill my life's mission which is:

To teach people how to become financially independent thru sound financial planning. To teach others how to grow their money in the simplest possible way and to teach people how they can grow as a person so that they can in turn influence others in a positive way.

All of us hope or should I say, dream of getting rich but not everybody is lucky enough to have their dreams fulfilled. Fortunately for me, I got interested in reading books. One day, I encountered a subject about financial planning and from then on, I allotted a lot of time in studying this subject. I've read tons of books and attended various seminars about financial subjects and personal development. From these, I discovered that there is a way to become rich which has proven to be effective by many if followed well and practiced diligently.

I've learned that most self-made millionaires have failed over and over again before they finally found their true success in life. And whatever they did, I too can achieve if I will try hard enough.

This book is about concepts and strategic steps on how to have freedom from financial problems, understanding money and how it works, making money work for you in attaining your personal goals and performing your life's mission and purpose. This is a concept on how to stop slaving for money your whole lifetime and in the end, still end up with no money.

After graduating from high school, my best friend June dragged me to enroll in B.S. Marine Transportation; a course you need to get if you wanted to be a seaman. He convinced me to take the course on the promise that after graduation his uncle, who was, at that time soon to be ship Captain, would take care of us and help us board a ship. Afraid of going to college alone (my real dream was to become a doctor] and losing my best friend's company, I agreed even though I knew that it was a huge gamble on my part for I did not have the faintest idea about the life and work of a seaman nor did I have a single seaman as a relative. Especially at that time, it was very difficult to board a ship unless you had a relative to back you up.

After graduating from college, things did not happen according to plan. I took care of myself in finding a job as seaman and I was hired immediately on the merit of my scholastic records. I knew that the only way I was going to finish college after high school was to be a scholar and I maintained my good grades to keep my scholarship.

Working on board a ship is not an easy task. As a ship's crew you will experience almost every kind of job. You can be a janitor, a carpenter, a painter, even a line man like the line men of Meralco who climb the posts, and many other job descriptions that the officers on the ship will require you to do. Aboard ship you must be ready to do anything and everything to keep the ship afloat.

Most parents think that being a seaman is just a walk in the park, and that all you have to do is pick up dollars at every corner of the ship and bring it home. It made the maritime course very attractive to those parents wanting an easy way out of poverty. They then send their children to maritime schools in the hope that one day they will be rich. In exchange for that, their son or daughter will spend their entire life working on board a ship. It is for this reason that today even a medical school is now offering a maritime course because they see the opportunity of making money by offering seaman's courses even if they are not qualified to do it.

After learning about this thing called financial planning and personal growth, it became my life's mission to teach my fellow seamen and OFWs (Overseas Filipino Workers] on how to become financially independent thru sound financial planning, how they too can grow their money in the simplest way possible and how they can also grow as a person so that they can influence others positively.

I've seen a lot of seamen and OFWs who have worked their whole life abroad only to find out that in the end they have nothing to show for it. Many of them were not even able to build their own houses and now live their retirement lives at the mercy of their children. Not to mention that most of them have not developed good family relationships due to the fact that most of their lives were spent abroad working to earn dollars and thus had less time to spend for their families. It's so sad.

As I am not a writer, I knew then that if I wrote this book, I run the risk of committing grammatical and typographical errors as the English language is not my strongest point. But I strongly felt that I should nevertheless go ahead and write this book, not only for my fellow OFWs but also for the many others who I believe, this material would be useful for them in finding their way to financial independence and life's success. I will try to discuss this matter in the simplest manner possible to be understood by anybody. Even professional like attorneys, accountants and even bankers have the same problems with finances as we do. And a vast majority of them are in deep trouble like most ordinary Filipino families, so don't lose hope.

This book is divided into three parts.

In part one, we will discuss how to grow your money and the different tools we can use in order to achieve this.

Part two of this book is about the steps in achieving financial independence. It may not be precise but the vast majority of financial planners and motivational speakers will surely agree with me.

After discussing how to grow and handle your money and the steps to achieve financial independence, part three will talk about how you yourself can grow at the same rate that your money grows and how to become more effective as a person. For what is money without finding the true meaning of a good life?

What you are about to learn can change your life, only if you are ready and prepared for a new way of living the things you've always done when you wake up. Victor Hugo once said "There is no greater idea whose time has come." I don't know what time it is at this point in your life but I hope that I've met you at the right time through this book.

If you're reading this book because you just want to check what I am trying to convey, then please do so. But after reading this and you find out that what I'm trying to teach is rational enough, I insist that you re-read it—again and again until you fully absorb the ideas. Please be warned that this is not a get-rich-quick guide book since I don't believe in an easy way out in life. Life is a journey where you have to be successful in learning what life teaches you everyday. I hope that this book will give you some insight on how to get your life's desire. As I said, the word rich and poor are relative and you will never know the difference until the moment you take hold of it and experience being rich.

Grow Your Money And Enjoy A Life Full of Abundance

PART I

GROW YOUR MONEY AND ENJOY A LIFE OF ABUNDANCE

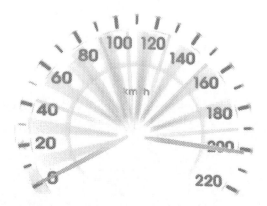

CHAPTER 1

THE FAST CHANGING WORLD

It is men who face the biggest problems in the future,
adjusting to their new and complicated role.
Anna Ford
British broadcaster
Remark

There are 365 days in a year, 24 hours in a day, 60 minutes in an hour and so on. A great thinker once said that we are living in a time wrap, that in order for us to stay in our current time, we have to revolve at the same rate as the earth does. Imagine this: the earth is an oblate spheroid or a round object in layman's terms. But why do people who live in the South Pole or even us who live in the Equator do not fall out of the earth? But if you get a ball and put an object on the bottom without putting glue, surely that object will fall. This is due to the fact that all of us are moving at the same rate as the earth does. This is elementary knowledge.

We are living in a fast paced and changing world that if we don't change at the same rate as the world around us, chances are we will perish. I'm not a Darwinian Theory believer that we originated from apes; I still choose to believe that God created man in His own image. I don't know with you but I'd choose to look like God than look like an ape. But some thesis of the Darwinian theory holds true that for us to outlive extinction we have to evolve and not suffer the same fate that happened to dinosaurs and other species that are extinct now. If you view evolution from a different perspective, true enough, everything evolves for the betterment in order for a thing or a being to survive.

Great changes have happened these past few years and this is a momentous point in time for the human race. We can expect that in the next few years, far more greater changes will emerge that if we fail to adapt, we will surely go the way of the caveman.

Some of the changes that are happening now are:

Before, travel to other countries was only possible by ship and it would take you weeks or even months depending on the distance of your destination. But now, you can travel around the whole world in just a few days or even go to outer space to enjoy your summer vacation.

Before, people communicated by drums, smoke signals or by the relaying of words using people stationed on high trees at regular intervals. This method changed when they discovered written communication and with it the beginning of recording events up until the courier system was developed. Morse code, which uses a series of dots and dashes to communicate was invented. Eventually, men discovered a way to communicate by means of radio wave signals.

Human beings, being impatient animals, were not satisfied with this limited version of communication. Alexander Graham Bell invented the telephone and eventually in the mid-1980s the first cellular phone was introduced in the market, and soon, Bill Gates achieved his dream of connecting people around the world using the personal computer or PC that can communicate not only by text or voice but even video too.

During my childhood, we used to watch movies at our neighbor's house. They were using Betamax tapes. Then came the VHS and the Long Playing Disc. But long before that, people used to watch movies that back then were played without sounds and with fast, clipped actions. I had several opportunities to see some of those movies when I was a kid. Some TV stations would play old movie clips from the past like Charlie Chaplain. Now you can even watch movies in your own cell phone.

Before, people listened to music by playing a vinyl record on their phonograph which was eventually replaced by the cassette tape. Now you can listen to your favorite music through your MP3 or MP4 player. Gadgets have become smaller and smaller and features have become more plentiful, not to mention the controls that are, more often than not, more intricate than before. Modern technology is at our own disposal.

It's good to see that humans are becoming more technologically sophisticated, but the question remains: "How are we going to deal with human problems?" Are we able to follow that same fast changing pace in finding solutions to one of the most important aspect of life—money problems?

True enough, the money we are receiving is increasing. If the inflow of money has increased, then why do we have to be frugal. We are prudent, but why is it that in the end, we still don't have money?

Today we can say that working hard is not enough, though this was the formula of success of our great grandparents. Gone were the days that having a land to till with was enough to raise twelve children. Nowadays, those twelve children are fighting with one another on who will take the responsibility of caring for the parents. Before, having a secure job in a good company guaranteed a leisurely retirement. But now, job security is a thing of the past due to mergers, acquisitions, mass layoffs and contractualization. You may have just been hired, but on your first day in the job, you're already worrying on what company you will apply to after six months.

Before, having a good profession, like being a doctor, guaranteed wealth but now doctors are becoming nurses or worse, care givers. I remember watching a television program that featured a doctor who had just passed the licensure board exam. It was so depressing to learn that he was again studying to become a nurse in the U.S. And you know the irony of that story? He was the top notcher among the examinees who took that medical board exam that year! Before, nurses continued studying to become doctors, but now it's the other way around with doctors studying again to become nurses, which is quite degrading. With this development, it's now more expensive to be a registered nurse than to be a doctor of medicine. A lot of parents have succumbed to the temptation of the possibility of earning dollars that they push their children to become nurses. However, after investing huge amounts in tuition fees and even after passing the board exams, many nursing graduates end up in call centers.

Changing worlds require changing solutions. This is so true in the area of money matters. Maybe working hard was applicable to the problems during our grandparents' time. But now, financial knowledge is the way to financial freedom.

Several years ago, a very interesting study was conducted. According to this study, they studied 100 young people aged 25 and tracked these people 40 years later or at their retirement age of 65. They discovered the following situations:

36 had already died which means that only 64 of them were still living. Out of 64, how many of them wanted to be rich? Of course if you asked them, ALL of them definitely wanted to be rich, but did all of them really become rich? NO! So what happened?

- Only 1 become wealthy
- 4 were financially independent
- 5 were still working because they needed to.
- And the overwhelming majority, 54, was financially broke.

Where would you want to be in that statistic? Whether you like it or not, the answer would depend heavily on the level of your financial education.

The moment I realized this, the first thing I did was to set aside a budget for my financial education. Most people think that financial education is expensive, so they opted to be ignorant on that subject matter. But Mark Victor Hansen said it well. "Poverty is a degrading, dehumanizing, cancer-like disease of the uninformed mind."

When I was young and I started to realize that me and my Mom were very poor, I started to hate my life. We lived in a very depressed community and I did not even know the meaning of the word squatters, for that was how they called us. At first I didn't know that we were poor, until I entered elementary school that I started to compare my life condition with my other classmates.

Then came the conflict in my mind, I started to hate everything around me; my environment, my playmates, my mother and myself and yes, even God. Whenever I prayed, I always asked Him why He gave me such a difficult and downtrodden life. I wondered why we couldn't choose who our parents can be once we were born.

I became blind to what my mother had done, to all the things she sacrificed and went through in order for us to survive. I never realized how lucky I was to have her. I distinctly remember an incident when I was about five years old, when she was about to eat a certain food, I grabbed that from her and she only meekly allowed me to have it.

I developed an enormous envy for my other classmates who had better life conditions than me. I cursed my situation whenever I opened my lunch box at school, If I was lucky, I would find rice with fried egg, if not I would find nothing. While my classmate had fancy sandwiches, if they had rice it came with either a hotdog, bacon and such, but never an egg. One day I felt a sudden joy in my heart and started thinking what if I pretended that I am rich.

From then on I always daydreamed that I am rich. One time my aunt got so annoyed with me because she saw me eating "tuyo" (dried salted fish] with a spoon and fork which was normally eaten with bare hands. I said that this is how rich people eat. It become my commitment to be rich. Though it's sad that for most people, when they succumb to the temptation of working hard to become rich, they forget the joy of dreaming and visualization. You dream at the beginning and when the dream begins to become reality, you take control but unfortunately later on your dream controls you.

It is useless to blame your parents or anyone else including yourself, about your present condition today. But it is time to end this poverty. It is time to decide that you will be financially free now. It is time for you to be free from the role of a victim.

THE FINANCIAL SEE SAW

Most people get a fair amount of fun out of their lives, but on balance, life is suffering and only the very young or the very foolish imagine otherwise.
George Orwell
Shooting an Elephant, "Lear, Tolstoy and the Fool"

Life is a continuous seeking for constant balance. When I was in high school every subject that we studied taught us about different things in balancing; balancing of chemical formulas in chemistry, balancing of forces in physics, balancing of time and attitude in values education, and balancing of the economy and its indicators in our economics subject. We studied those subjects without even asking ourselves the relevance of these things in life. After being taught numerous things about balancing, I wondered why we are not able to apply it and balance our lives when it comes to having problems versus solutions especially in the area of finances.

One day I was walking in our subdivision's park where the clubhouse was and also where the playground was located. I watched as some kids joyously played traditional Filipino games such as "piko and luksong-tinik" while others were just running around. At the corner of the playground I noticed two small kids around ages of five playing see-saw. I watched them until my mind roamed around, until the idea about balancing came alive.

Life is not balanced as we think. Like a see-saw, that whenever one side is elevated, the other should come down or else it would come to the point that both end are stuck in the middle and waiting for who will make the first move. But whatever the situation is whether end point A or B is up; the sum of two opposing ends should sum up into one.

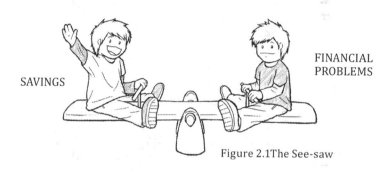

SAVINGS

FINANCIAL PROBLEMS

Figure 2.1The See-saw

All of us belong to the same statistic we call life. Whatever our life situation is right now, we take a part of the whole pie which is usually cut into two major parts; sad or happy, success or failure, good or bad, even rich or poor. If one part is small then the other will be large, the sum of the two is always the whole of the parts. This is life's duality. We have seen things as two different entities but in reality they are both part of a whole. But the proportion and mixture of it is what makes life exciting. Like night there is day, but night and day does not mean that they always have an equal part. The length of the day seems to be equal for us living in the equatorial area. But ask the people who live near the Poles how long their days are during summer and how short it is during winter.

I remember when one of my aunts complained to me about my cousin who was about my age. She lamented on how disappointed she was because my cousin was bad. Then after her long story of agony I told her that maybe my cousin was not really a bad person after all but he just did not have enough reason to be good.

In financial statistics everybody has an equal opportunity but not all of us can be rich. And from the beginning, the rich are always less than the poor in numbers; but in power the other way is true.

In personal finance the same thing holds true. Our financial responsibility or financial freedom is inversely proportional to the money that we have saved. As our savings line goes up; our financial problem goes down and vice versa. We can expect to lessen our financial problem the moment we start keeping or saving and managing our money. And as a general rule as we grow old we should expect to be more financially free, but most of the time that is not the case. The bitter reality is, as we grow old the more money problems we have and the more financially insecure we feel even if we try to earn more.

Going back to our see-saw analogy, if we think that our financial condition is like a see-saw, putting our savings on one end and financial problem on the other, we must control how it moves and bear in mind that we are responsible to whatever outcome it would give.

SAVINGS

FINANCIAL PROBLEMS

SAVINGS

FINANCIAL
PROBLEMS

Figure 2.2A
See-saw with heavy
financial problems

If we want to be financially free, we can do it by slowly putting more load on our savings. Financial problems become heavier when our savings decreases (Fig. 2.2A) and conversely, whenever our savings increase; our financial problems become lighter and we become financially free and more financially secure. (Fig. 2.2B)

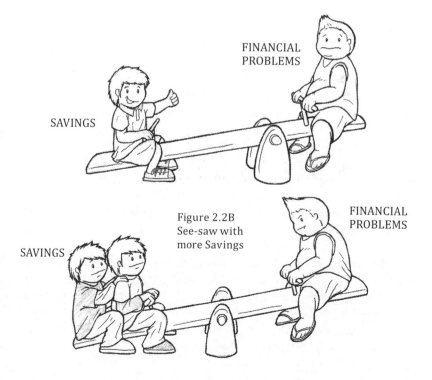

FINANCIAL
PROBLEMS

SAVINGS

Figure 2.2B
See-saw with
more Savings

FINANCIAL
PROBLEMS

SAVINGS

As I have said, as we grow old we should have accumulated more and more savings as we are working. When we were a child we did not have much power over our finances, for we are entirely dependent on our parents. Why is it that the moment we start to have our own source of income, our financial problems or challenges become much greater than our savings?

If we neglect to plan for our finances, the harder we will work for the money, the more financial problems we will be facing. Things will get even worse when we start to have a family of our own. Then along comes our children that make things even more complicated. And when we fail to teach them about finances, the moment they have a family of their own we will take care, not only of them but also the new family they will have. Consequently we will be facing more troubles than we have ever dreamed about. If nobody among them takes charge of their life, the vicious cycle of financial disasters will start anew.

If we can prepare for our future and start accumulating savings for our various financial needs, financial problems should start to decrease. This is what I'm referring to, that as we grow old, our savings should increase and conversely, our financial obligations should also decrease. This is especially true when our children finish college; this is the time when we should start to feel free.

But in most Filipino families this is not always the case. As we age the more financial obligations we face. This is one of the consequences of the lack of financial education. Nobody taught us in school about this thing called financial literacy. We learn money matters by just merely observing our parents.

If we will try to observe ourselves and how we deal with money, you will notice that it is a direct reflection of how our parents' example on money matters. If you are having trouble in dealing with financial issues then just look back on how you picked up these things from your parents and maybe by then you can start doing something to remedy the situation.

I have a very close family friend, Bernando. He and his wife, Tina have nine children. I vividly remember the time when they only had two; they lived in full abundance. Bernardo and Tina failed to look forward for their financial needs. Whatever they earned they literally spent everything and most of the time they were in debt—unnecessary debt. Since they are spending most of what they are earning they would always fight and it was always about money issues. They blamed each other but failed to notice that they both had problems with it. I also noticed that whenever they fought heavily, a new baby was born afterwards, until such time they stopped fighting they were surprised to realize that they already have nine children.

But looking back when they still had a small family, they enjoyed a life of abundance. They were able to buy things that they wanted and whenever their kids celebrate their birthdays, they did it with a real bang. But when the children started to go to school, things changed dramatically; they got deeper and deeper in debt and eventually started selling their properties piece by piece.

Their problems could have been avoided had they learned to manage their life in the way they wanted it and the same also holds true in regards with their money problems.

But the brutal reality of life is this: when will we learn? After every misfortune that happens to us, we just accept defeat, hoping that in the next life—if there is one, we will not suffer the same fate, then we slouch on our sofa holding a bottle of beer on one hand and contemplating how unfair life is while watching our favorite tele-novela.

THE TWO SOURCES OF INCOME

Are we interested in treating the symptoms of poverty and economic stagnation through income redistribution and class warfare, or do we want to go at the root causes of poverty and economic stagnation by promoting pro-growth policies that promote prosperity?

Paul Ryan

Modern dictionaries define money as the medium of exchange issued by a government or other public authorities in the form of coins, gold, silver, or other metal, or paper bills, *used as the measure of the value* of goods and services.

It means that money is equal to the value that we are willing to give either in the form of goods or services.

MONEY=VALUE

Whatever value we give is equal to the amount of money we receive. Money is also used to barter for something which has an equal value to our money. For example if you want to buy a hamburger and you know that the value of one hamburger is P50, definitely you're not going to pay P500 for it, that's not logical.

So, therefore, the secret to riches is to simply increase our value. Meaning, if your income is not enough for your wants and needs, it means you only need to increase your value. Increase the value of your time by taking a part time job, part time business or home based business. Increase the value of your performance in your current job for you to be promoted. Then as you climb the ladder of success in your career, money naturally follows, or increase the value of your money by investing it.

The moment I understood the concept of value I stopped blaming my current life situation and for not having what I want. I stopped cursing my parents and the environment where I grew up. I even started having a deeper relationship with God. Remember life will not give you what you want or what you need. Life gives you what you deserve not what you think you deserve, and what you deserve is based on how valuable you are in the market place.

In the same manner, after eating tons of junk foods and feeling sluggish, you cannot just say to the good Lord, "give me wellness and long life"—No! On the other hand you might say; "I am a good citizen of this country, I pay my bills on time, I attend Sunday mass regularly, can I become a successful person?" Still No! The answer is; develop yourself to become a deserving person you want to be. And this is what is amazing, if you become a deserving fellow you don't even need to ask anybody for the things you need in life.

There are two sources of income that most financial planners agree on; the active income and the passive income.

Active Income is the return we receive for our labors; that is our salary or wage; it's like selling your time in return for the money. The more time you can sell the more income you will receive. Some call this as linear income. If your source of income is active income then whoever pays you, owns your time and can ask you to do whatever they want to, for as long as your time is being paid. We become a "wage slave". If the person who's paying you doesn't want your time anymore and if active income is your only source then definitely you'll beg them to keep you on their payroll, or else you'll need to find another person who's interested with your time. In this situation you are at their mercy. The moment you stop using your time you stop receiving money. Even if you are working as a top executive of a major company which pays high rates of remuneration, as soon as you stop working, money stops flowing.

Meanwhile passive income is the profit of our money which works for us. It means that our own money is working for us.

"How can money work for me if I don't have it?" Then you must have an active income first, while earning you must let your income produce another income. You must buy things that will produce money not things that "eats money". It's like buying a "Money Making Machine"

Why is it important that money work for us? Money, unlike human beings, never gets tired of working. With man, the money is only equal with the time he works, the more time he works, the more money he can produce. But with money working, it can work

24 hours a day, 7 days a week. I don't know with you but for me I can't work at that pace.

Has your banker ever called to inform you that your money has asked for a sick leave? That's another good thing with money it never gets sick. On the contrary, when it is working for us and we happen to get sick, it can be of assistance to us. Try to go to your nearest hospital without it and you'll realize how important money is.

Like most of us passive income has a big brother—residual income. It is same with passive income that money is working for you and addicted to time. Residual income is a little bit sophisticated and clever for it is using the time of other people. Wow! But don't worry, for it works in a mutual relationship. You don't only get the income that your money earned but you are giving also other people a chance to earn their own income by providing them a job. In so doing you get a percentage of their income.

This happens when you own a business and somebody is operating it, meaning you can sleep while your business is rolling. If you are the one operating your own business it is an active income. You cannot consider yourself a businessman but rather a self employed man, like a dentist who owns his or her clinic, or a technician who has a shop. Since it is an active income it requires your time, the more money you want the more time you must allocate in giving services and management.

Participating in network-marketing programs is a good example of residual income. At first you need to establish your network, but the moment your own network starts working on its own, you will receive a residual income to their work done.

The good thing with network marketing is, you don't have to give your full time just a part of your time. Just imagine if you can give a part of your time for let's say four hours a day, then you will able to recruit people who are also willing to give four hours of their time. Just imagine the moment it takes off, how many hours you will have in one day if everybody is recruiting and giving four hours each. It is called time leveraging.

A word of caution: you have to be careful in choosing a network-marketing company for many are fraudulent who hide behind a network-marketing form. Choose a company whose products tell a story and offer good training programs for network-marketing is a good way to enhance your selling ability and a way to start your own small business.

When I first joined a network-marketing business which sold natural health products, a lot of people were surprised. For it is very uncommon for a seaman especially whose rank on board ship is Chief Mate to hear making sales talk about networking.

At first I was hesitant in doing it, but when I started to appreciate the products it offered, I decided to give it a try. After all, who doesn't want an extra cash flow? Then after just a few months, my efforts started to pay off. I was able to have a longer vacation off-ship as my income from my network-marketing through selling and recruiting paid for all my wants and needs while having a vacation. And by being a part timer of that business, I was able to acquire my first car.

When all this happened, the people who didn't believe in me at first, started to follow. Every time I was on board ship, I introduced this business system to my fellow shipmates. I appreciate it more when my residual income starts to flow in. Even when I'm on board the ship sailing to different parts of the world, my groups or what we call downlines are working and as they are earning so do I.

To differentiate more, here are examples of active and passive income and what they require.

Active Income	Requires	Passive Income	Requires
Seaman/OFW	Contract	Interest on Investment	Savings
Local Worker	Contract	Income from Franchise	Product Ideas
Doctors	Patients	Income from Network Marketing	Part Time
Technician	Troubled Machines	Income from Business	Good Manager
Actors	Movie Projects		

Table 2.1 Difference between Active and Passive Income

Our basic needs like food, shelter, clothing, education and health care are provided by our income, be it passive or active. It also pays for our debts and obligations to other people. Financial freedom can be defined by the ability of our resources to pay for our wants and needs by the way we choose to live. And these resources must come from your passive income, for what is greater than living a life you choose without even working at all.

But if we are living in the income that other people are giving us or by being wage-slaves, we are less secure. Just imagine when your salary stops, are you going to stop eating? Would you have the guts to walk on the streets naked? Can you live without your shelter? Can you stop sending your children to school? Maybe you can, but what promises will their future bring? Will you just wait until you die when you get sick?

Remember this, no matter how big your salary is from your job, it's useless if you don't have a passive income. I do not criticize people who are employed for I myself am an employee too. But it must be our long term financial goal that one day we can rest and let our money work for us. Start building your passive income and let your money be your slave not the other way around.

Someone asked: how can I make money if in the first place I don't have any. This is the problem that most of us have for we are raised with the idea that for you to make money you first need to have money. We often mistake that money is the only form of capital. Yes it's true that you make money thru buy and sell, after all that's the fastest way to make money. But don't discount the possibility that it is also possible for you to make money by doing sell and buy, and if you do that way you don't need money to start a business.

One day you go to your friend and tell a story of how wonderful the products you have encountered. You made a very effective sales presentation to the point that your friend asks you, how can I have one of those products? Then you explain to him that you can do it for him but the only problem is you don't have money to cover for it. That if he trusts you enough you can get it for him by asking for his money with a little mark-up for your effort. Then true enough your friend trusted you and you made money out of that deal. If you were able to do it once, do you think you can do it again, the answer is definitely YES. Ingenuity and creativity is the most effective form of capital, it's not always money. So you don't need money to make money.

THE CHALLENGES IN FINANCIAL PLANNING

Planning is as natural to the process of success as its absence is to the process of failure.
Robin Sieger

All financial planning no matter how you do it, focuses on two major financial problems—dying too soon or living too long. Whenever I ask people to choose which they prefer, they always choose the latter, though in reality both are problems that we must be prepared for.

Dying too soon. What will be your problem with it? You will have no problem because you are six feet below the ground, but the family that you left behind will suffer. How can you have problem when you are not even aware of what is happening to your family; whether they are still eating, still having a house to live in or will your children still be studying. If you can see them suffering because of the adverse situation your sudden death placed them in, can you serenely claim the word written on top your grave: RIP [Rest In Peace]?

So what is the solution to that kind of financial problem?—PROTECTION. Protect your income by having insurance. The moment you start to have a family of your own and become a breadwinner, life insurance is very important for you to have.

How about living too long? Is there any problem with that? If you have money it may not be a problem at all. But if you live until age 90 or even 100 without money to support your needs much less your wants, let alone the increasing need for medical attention, then you are in deep trouble.

Remember, during your working days you rely on your salary to live, when you retire and stop working your income stops and all the benefits of being an employee also stop. Though some will say that this is not a problem for they regularly give contributions to their social security. Ask the retiree how much they are receiving from SSS or GSIS as pension and you will find how disappointing it is. Not to mention the delays it takes before the check lands in the retiree's hand.

So what is the solution to that second financial problem?—INVESTMENT. Invest a small portion of your income regularly not only for your varied financial goal but as well as for your golden retirement year. The earlier you start setting aside for your retirement the cheaper it will cost you. A lot of people commit the mistake by assuming that when they retire their expenses will become smaller compared to what they used to have when they are actively working. Look at the senior citizens who are a regular patients of diuretic clinics and ask them how expensive each visit to that treatment center is.

The problem is that most young people don't care about retirement when you explain it to them because they erroneously think that there is still a lot of time to plan for that. Until one day they wake up and realize that everything is already too late. **Do you want to know the secret to financial disaster?**

PLANNING YOUR RETIREMENT WHEN YOU'RE RETIRED.

CHAPTER 2

SAVINGS LEVERAGE

We buy things we don't need.
With money we don't have.
To impress people we don't like.

To achieve a certain level of financial security, the biggest challenge now is how to make Side A [Savings] weigh more than Side B [Financial Problems] of the Financial See Saw analogy that we have discussed in Chapter 1. One way is through Savings Leverage. Savings Leverage is having a life insurance policy to cushion life's financial obligations in the event of the unexpected death of the person who's in charge of increasing Side A, the savings side.

This is one of the Philippines' major problems because only a few people understand the value of life insurance. Whenever they were approached by an insurance agent and asked to buy life insurance for themselves, they immediately decline without giving any second thought about their decision.

Most of us think that having life insurance is like preparing for your own death. Even some think that this issue is too taboo to be discussed. Since most of us were not taught the value of financial planning in school, what more about the importance of life insurance? The moment we experience financial difficulties, guess which one is the first thing we are not going to pay?— Insurance premiums! Where in fact this is the most critical time that we should keep ourselves insured, for if something should happen during our financial difficulty, at least we have insurance that will cushion our family from financial obscurity. We fail to appreciate the value of life insurance.

As I write this book, only 4% of the Filipino population has private insurance and a vast majority of this 4% don't understand their policies or they may not be adequately protected, for they bought that insurance just to make the agent stop stalking them. Most of them bought their life insurance policies without even knowing how much life insurance they really need or why they need it at all.

Life insurance is like renting a house. When you don't have a house, you have to rent a place for yourself for you to have a place to live in. Why rent? Because at the present time, you cannot build your own home yet with your current income or savings. But your life goal is to have your own house one day. The same with savings, if you don't have enough savings to consider yourself financially free, then you have to "rent" savings. That's what we call savings leverage.

Having life insurance is like renting money for a much cheaper price, if you don't have enough savings in your current condition, then having insurance is a wise move.

That's why it is so important to do a financial need analysis first before you buy any insurance to make sure you are properly protected. I suggest you talk to your financial planner to know how much coverage you really need. But as a general rule you need to have at least ten times of your annual gross income to be properly protected. What does it mean? It means for your family to be protected in the event of your sudden loss, you must have that enough savings which is ten times your gross annual income. But if you don't have that savings yet, then that's the time you need to have life insurance, to supplement the financial needs of your family.

It is very important for the bread winner to be properly protected because one of the purposes of insurance is income continuation, meaning we can lose the bread winner but not his income. Then the moment you have attained the savings you need then maybe insurance is then optional for you. Just like a house, why rent when you have your own.

Let's take for example the case of Maria Theresa who was an engineer and so her husband Lito. One day Maria Theresa was approached by an insurance agent and discussed with her the importance of life insurance. She got interested in buying insurance for herself and for her husband when she learned how important it is. She invited the agent to her home one weekend, so her husband could hear also what she had learned. When the agent arrived, she called her husband who was busy talking to someone on the phone. But when her husband learned that it was about insurance he immediately dismissed the agent by saying "Insurance? I don't have time for that!"

Maria Theresa felt embarrassed by her husband's behavior, and because of this she told the agent to just meet her again at her office. To cut the long story short Maria Theresa bought life insurance for herself.

Two years later Maria Theresa suffered a heart attack, was rushed to the emergency room but did not survive. When the agent learned about it, she talked to Theresa's secretary to prepare the necessary documents needed to process the claim.

The agent visited the wake of Maria Theresa bringing a mass card with her. The agent approached Lito and asked him if he still remember her. Lito replied that he seems to. The agent said: "I am the agent who was invited by your wife one weekend in your house to discuss life insurance. But you told us that you did not have time for life insurance. But Maria Theresa loved you so much that she bought a life insurance policy worth P20 million. Now Lito, may I ask you? Do you have time for 20 million?"

Life insurance is much cheaper for younger people, because as you grow old it becomes more expensive with the assumption that you are nearing the time that you will use it. Another fact of life insurance is; when you don't need it, it's very cheap but when the time comes that you need it badly then it becomes very expensive or worse, nobody will sell to you anymore.

USES OF LIFE INSURANCE

When the middle classes, feeling poor, wring their hands
and wonder what it is the working classes don't spend
money on . . . one of the answers is—insurance.
Katharine Whitehorn
How to Survive Your Money
Problems, "Insurance"

1. Income Continuation

"Unless one is wealthy there is no use in being a charming fellow.
Romance is the privilege of the rich, not the profession of the unemployed.
The poor should be practical and prosaic. It is better to
have a permanent income than to be fascinating."
Oscar Wilde
(Irish Poet, Novelist, Dramatist
and Critic. 1854-1900)

Elmer was a very successful business owner; he had a thriving export garment factory and his three children were just starting to go to school. His wife, Elvira was a plain house wife and had little interest or knowledge about the business. Since they were successful at that time, nobody could get near them unless they knew them personally, much more a life insurance agent who was dying to sell them life insurance for they were very good prospects.

One day Elmer discovered that his business was almost bankrupt because his business partner, who was also his best friend, had swindled him. He could not accept the truth that he suffered a heart attack and in less than a week, he died.

It was a very catastrophic event for Elvira for she was alone in this situation. Elmer, having no life insurance left his family a mountain of debt that forced Elvira to declare bankruptcy and go back to her province to live a simpler life.

In the province she met a life insurance agent who discussed with her the importance of life insurance. After learning the importance of insurance she cried and asked the agent: "Why in hell did you not come at the time we needed you most!" With that experience, Elvira decided to became a financial planner to help others avoid suffering the same fate as hers.

Before buying any life insurance, it's very important that you must first know how much you really need and how much your current savings is. One of the uses of life insurance is to make sure that even in the unexpected death of the bread winner of the family his or her dependents will still be able to continue to get their basic needs; and to enjoy the things that they used to have when their provider was still around.

In the case of my friend Carlos, he had a monthly salary of P30,000, so it means that in one year he could earn P360,000. For him to protect his income, he needs P7,200,000. It means that his savings must have that same amount. To justify this, here is our computation. We are going to assume that Carlos will invest his money for a fix income that would give him an annual yield of 5%.

Therefore:

P30,000 x 12(mo.] = 360,000 / 5% = P7,200,000

Why so huge you might ask. A lot of people who have benefitted from life insurance made terrible mistakes. The moment they receive the benefits, in less than a year or two years at the most, everything is gone. This is wrong because the purpose of life insurance is income continuation.

What Carlo's family should do is re-invest the money that would give them a fix income of as per our assumption 5%. Therefore:

P7,200,000 x 5% = 360,000 (annually] or P30,000 (monthly)

It means that if Carlos' family would follow the same strategy and even if Carlos has long been gone, his family would not be crippled by the tragic event. This is especially true when they still have young children to look after and will eventually need to send them to school.

Whatever savings Carlos has, can be deducted to his insurance need, for that savings could be included to the fund that must be re-invested as per the above suggestion. Going back to our See Saw analogy, we could illustrate it in three scenarios; if Carlos has 1 million savings, 5 million savings or 7.2million savings.

P1Million
SAVINGS

P6.2
Million

FINANCIAL
PROBLEMS

Figure 3.1A. When Carlos has 1 Million savings

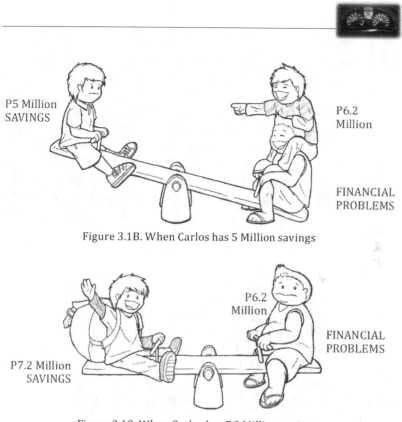

P5 Million
SAVINGS

P6.2
Million

FINANCIAL
PROBLEMS

Figure 3.1B. When Carlos has 5 Million savings

P6.2
Million

FINANCIAL
PROBLEMS

P7.2 Million
SAVINGS

Figure 3.1C. When Carlos has 7.2 Million savings
equal to his needs. Point of equilibrium

In figure 3.1C, Carlos reached his savings equal to his insurance need, this is the point where insurance is just an option to him. As we have said like a house why rent when you have your own.

There is another thing to consider in buying insurance, know which one is suitable for you, whether it is Term insurance or Whole Life Insurance.

Term insurance is the cheapest life insurance product because it will protect you for a certain duration only; whether it be 1 yr, 5 yrs, 10 yrs or until age 65. What is its advantage? Since it is the cheapest it means you could buy your life insurance need right away without sacrificing your other financial needs. The downside is when you outlive your insurance coverage you will not get anything from it. This is a pure protection only.

While Whole Life Insurance will protect you until age 100, its price depends on its product features. It is more expensive than Term Insurance for it has a savings component. Meaning, you are giving extra money to the Insurance Company to invest it for you. But of course, whatever earning your savings get, the insurance company will take a major part of it in consideration of their effort in making your money earn. With Whole Life Insurance you will get the Face Value of your insurance plus the earnings of its savings component when you outlive your insurance coverage.

So what is best for you? It will depend on your personal needs. The most effective way is to get both types of insurance. Get a whole life insurance to protect you and your projected assets once you retire. During your prime years, you will produce and accumulate a lot of assets; your insurance protection must then be sufficient to protect those assets. The difference between your insurance needs when you retire to your insurance needs during your prime years could then be augmented by having term insurance.

Another approach is, if you think you have the ability to do your own way of investing your money then do so. This will give you a bigger opportunity in terms of yields on your investment than entrusting your extra money to a life insurance company. Just make sure that you have enough coverage at least with term insurance. In this case having term insurance will give you excess money that you can add to your investment because term insurance is relatively cheaper than whole life insurance.

Is it a bad idea to get too much insurance protection? No, not at all, after all insurance is also a form of investment. But you must remember that since it is a form of secure investment, your money could earn more if you will invest it on other investment vehicle once you know you have enough insurance. Again I suggest you talk to your financial planner on this matter.

2. Forced Savings

Never spend your money before you have it.
Thomas Jefferson

The Forced Savings feature of life insurance will take place if you buy whole life insurance. It has an ability to increase your insurance coverage and savings at the same time.

Having life insurance is one good form of saving especially for young people who are just starting to earn. Most of them will just indulge in buying gadgets and unnecessary things that lose value over time. Having life insurance as a form of savings is good for them for once they stop paying for it and the policy lapses then they will feel sorry for themselves for losing all that they have paid for. So the tendency is that they will be forced to save monthly to pay for their insurance premiums. In life insurance once you've stopped paying for it, it will soon lapse although you have an option to re-instate the policy within two years from the time it lapses, but still you have to pay a certain amount of penalty charges.

Here is a situation to exemplify the importance of savings and the value of starting as early as possible.

Mike started saving at age 25 but since his income was not big at that time, he was only able to save P25,000 annually. He saved it regularly by setting aside his savings first before he spent on anything. He did not deprive himself of doing things he wanted and buying what he liked but he also made sure that he did not fail to save a small amount of his income. Mike stopped saving at age 33 for he had to help his siblings study in college.

On the other hand Myla started saving at age 35. She started 10 years after Mike for her office peers often pressured her to always go with them in every gimmick they wanted; they were able to travel to various places in the Philippines as well as in some parts of Asia. When Mike told her about his savings scheme she was inspired so she began saving the same amount, P25,000 annually. Being Myla's boyfriend, their love bloomed so much that they set a date for their marriage.

When Mike and Myla reached the age 37, they got married. Since Myla still kept her job, she was able to continue her savings while Mike stopped at age 33. He still kept his savings invested though he was not able to add anything to it.

When they reached the age of 65 they retired. On that same year Myla stopped her savings.

In summary Mike was able to save P25,000 every year for eight year starting at age 25 while Myla saved the same amount every year for thirty years. The question now is, between them, who would have the bigger amount of retirement money?

When both of them went to the investment company were they placed their money, they were informed that their savings gave them a yield of 8% per annum. Guess who got more? Surprisingly it was Mike! Mike, who was only able to save for eight years before stopping, got P3,640,421 while Myla who saved for thirty years until her retirement, got only P3,330,338. There was a difference of P310,083. It may seem like a rather small amount but the big difference is the amount they actually saved. Mike saved only P200,000 while Myla saved P750,00

For those who want proof, here is what happened:

AGE	Mike's Investment	Mike's Total Money	Myla's Investment	Myla's Total Money
25	25,000	27,000.00	0	0
26	25,000	56,160.00	0	0
27	25,000	87,652.00	0	0
28	25,000	121,665.02	0	0
29	25,000	158,398.23	0	0

AGE	Mike's Investment	Mike's Total Money	Myla's Investment	Myla's Total Money
30	25,000	198,070.08	0	0
31	25,000	240,915.69	0	0
32	25,000	287,188.95	0	0
33	0	310,164.06	0	0
34	0	334,977.19	0	0
35	0	361,775.36	25,000	27,000.00
36	0	390,717.39	25,000	56,160.00
37	0	421,974.78	25,000	87,652.80
38	0	455,732.76	25,000	121,665.02
39	0	492,191.39	25,000	158,398.23
40	0	531,566.70	25,000	198,070.08
41	0	574,092.03	25,000	240,915.69
42	0	620,019.39	25,000	287,188.95
43	0	669,620.95	25,000	337,194.06
44	0	723,190.62	25,000	391,137.19
45	0	781,145.87	25,000	449,428.16
46	0	843,529.54	25,000	512,382.41
47	0	911,011.90	25,000	580,373.01
48	0	983,892.86	25,000	653,802.58
49	0	1,062,604.29	25,000	733,107.08
50	0	1,147,612.63	25,000	818,755.64
51	0	1,239,421.64	25,000	911,256.09
52	0	1,338,575.37	25,000	1,011,156.58
53	0	1,561.314.31	25,000	1,119,049.11
54	0	1,686,219.46	25,000	1,235,573.04
55	0	1,821,117.01	25,000	1,260,573.04
56	0	1,966,806.37	25,000	1,386,418.88
57	0	2,124,150.88	25,000	1,522,332.39
58	0	2,294,082.95	25,000	1,669,118.98
59	0	2,477,609.59	25,000	1,827,648.50
60	0	2,675,818.36	25,000	1,998,860.38

AGE	Mike's Investment	Mike's Total Money	Myla's Investment	Myla's Total Money
61	0	2,889,883.83	25,000	2,183,769.21
62	0	3,121,074.53	25,000	2,383,470.75
63	0	3,121,074.53	25,000	2,599,148.41
64	0	3,370,760.49	25,000	2,832,080.28
65	0	3,640,421.33	25,000	3,083,646.70
TOTAL AMT INVESTED	200,000		775,000	
TOTAL FUND UPON RETIREMENT		3,640,421.33		3,083,646.70

Table 3.1 Mike and Myla's Investment illustration

The above projection was based on 8% interest. What if your investment earned more than that? Another interesting thing was that Mike started at age 25. What more if Mike started at his teenage years? You might ask; "How can Mike save if he has no earnings on his teenage year?" Not true, we earn since childhood in one form or another. I'm sure you had a school allowance back then, that's a form of income. What if we taught our children the value of saving as early as childhood?

Life insurance will serve you the same purpose, as most life insurance products yield 8% to 14% annually and once you decide that you'd really need your money when you retire, you can have your policy liquidated if you think you don't need your life insurance policy anymore.

3. Estate Planning

The estate tax punishes years of hard work and robs families of part of their heritage by imposing a huge penalty on inheritance after death-a tax on money that has already been taxed.
Mike Fitzpatrick

Estate planning is not an easy task, one of the reasons that most ordinary Filipino people don't bother with it is because they don't understand this creature. Most of us think that being a good provider means providing your family a nice house giving your children access to good quality education is enough. But sorry to say it doesn't end there, though it's the beginning.

Alvin is a retired ship captain. After his retirement, he made himself busy by taking on a part time teaching position in one of the prestigious maritime schools in Manila. During his sea career, he and his family of six enjoyed a very comfortable life. He accumulated numerous assets during his seagoing years mostly investing in real estate.

But everything changed when one afternoon while preparing his lesson plan, Alvin suffered a massive heart attack and since no one was around at that time to help him, he died.

A week after Alvin was laid to rest, his family started discussing what had happened and what their next move would be after the departure of their beloved father. All of Alvin's unfinished business issues were discussed. There were properties to be transferred like; ownership of the house, the car, and his huge collection of real estate properties, and the bank account that was frozen until they could provide evidence that the estate tax was fully paid.

Alvin's family is now in great agony once again for they had to raise around P3.5 million, certainly a huge amount of money for them, for the settlement of the estate tax. If his family could not pay all the penalties and interests that had accumulated at a particular date, they were going to lose all of the assets that Alvin had worked and sacrificed so hard for in his lifetime.

Having a life insurance policy could have been one of the solutions that would have helped Alvin's family. But since he did not plan his finances well, he neglected to buy a life insurance policy and instead built up his assets in real properties. Alvin forgot to consider how he could make sure that what he built would be passed along to his next generation.

Buying a life insurance is a very good strategy for estate planning; it's like paying your estate tax at a very cheap price for a long period of time. And just in case the insured died too soon before the policy was fully paid, the policy will be considered fully paid. With that he can pass all of his assets to his loved ones without any trouble, provided that his insurance protection is sufficient for his financial needs.

To give you an idea about estate tax, as of writing, below is a table to show the current estate tax rate.

OVER	BUT NOT OVER	AMOUNT OF TAX	PLUS	OF EXCESS OVER
	200,000	EXEMPT		
200,000	500,000	0	5%	200,000
500,000	2,000,000	15,000	8%	500,000
2,000,000	5,000,000	135,000	11%	2,000,000
5,000,000	10,000,000	465,000	15%	5,000,000
10,000,000	And Over	1,215,000	20%	10,000,000

Table 3.2 Table of Estate Tax Rate

IF NET GIFT IS OVER	BUT NOT OVER	AMOUNT OF TAX	PLUS	OF EXCESS OVER
	100,000	EXEMPT		
100,000	200,000	0	2%	100,000
200,000	500,000	2,000	4%	200,000
500,000	1,000,000	14,000	6%	500,000
1,000,000	3,000,000	44,000	8%	1,000,000

IF NET GIFT IS OVER	BUT NOT OVER	AMOUNT OF TAX	PLUS	OF EXCESS OVER
3,000,000	5,000,000	204,000	10%	3,000,000
5,000,000	10,000,000	404,000	12%	5,000,000
10,000,000	And Above	1,004,000	15%	10,000,000

Table 3.3 Table of Donors Tax Rate

Sample Computation:

1. Estate tax

Total Net Estate: P 20,000,000

Tax: P 1,215,000 (Base on P10 mil]

```
  P 20,000,000
- P 10,000,000
  P 10,000,000
x          20%   —Rate in excess of P10 mil
  P  2,000,000
+ P  1,215,000
  P  3,215,000
```

2. Donor's Tax

Total Net Estate: P 20,000,000

Tax: P 1,004,000 (Base on P10 mil)

```
  P 20,000,000
- P 10,000,000
  P 10,000,000
x          15%   —Rate in excess of P10 mil
  P  1,500,000
+ P  1,004,000
  P  2,504,000
```

Imagine the huge chunk of money that will go to the government if your assets reach P20 million, it's P3,215,00. Although now our present estate tax rates have a lot of tax breaks but you still will have to consider this: the government will still get a big part of your estate later on.

Nevertheless, for some people who fully understand the consequences of huge estate taxes, they just give their properties to their heir while they are still living in the form of donation. Personally, I don't recommend it for we won't know what our health and financial conditions will be during our golden years. If you do such a thing, there might come a time when you would need your property to finance your current situation, but you cannot get it back because you've already given it to your children. And most of the time, it raises some family conflicts. Who will take care of you when everything you had was already given to somebody?

Even if you do consider that option; donating your estate with the same example of assets worth P20 million, it will still cost you P2,504,000. Although there is a much easier way in donation, you can do a staggered donation because tax is computed on how much you have donated in one year.

Sometimes it is one way of keeping your children always at your side while you are enjoying your retirement. Most of the children will be busy with their own lives that they will tend to forget their aging parents. Knowing that they still have their inheritance to expect from you it will surely remind them of their duties as affectionate sons and daughters.

4. Retirement Fund

The question isn't at what age I want to retire, it's at what income.
George Foreman

The most serious mistake one can make when it comes to financial planning is neglecting your financial needs for your retirement. Most of us don't bother about it until we reach that age, but sad to say retirement is not an option. Others think they don't need much during old age, they forget to factor in inflation when it comes to medicines and medical services, though it's correct to assume that maybe we might not need much of our other basic needs. But don't you think that it's a good idea to make yourself enjoy the fruit of your long years of labor by at least having a leisurely retirement?

Retirement would be much easier and inexpensive if you've planned it well in advance. It is the same thing with savings, the earlier you start, the earlier you can finish your required retirement fund.

In our country and our culture, this is one of the most neglected areas of money matters. When they retire, most people have no option but to live with their children and become their liability. The sad part of it is that most retirees will often hear from their children how they are becoming a burden and disturbance to their married life.

I have met an old man named Mario in one of the busy streets in Malate while having some snacks at a cafeteria. He approached me asking for some food and I bought him a sandwich. Since he looked harmless to me I asked him where he lived and if there is anybody taking care of him. I know it's a stupid question for if there was somebody's taking care of him he would not end up begging in the streets.

I've learned that he still had children but he didn't know where they lived now. His wife had been long gone since he was in his early forties. Since most of his children were also having difficulties with their lives he had no choice but to leave them alone to at least lessen their burden of providing for an old man. He left them not because he wanted to, but because he needed to, for everyday he always heard his children fighting among themselves about who's going to give him his allowance for the week. Now Mario felt so alone he doesn't know what tomorrow will bring him.

For sure he has no plan for that tomorrow, especially now that he's just living on a day to day basis.

It's so sad that after prioritizing our family during our prime years we end up alone in the end. This is how important retirement planning is.

Life insurance could be used for this purpose; there are some products of life insurance that will let you enjoy financial protection during your working years at the same time you can have it as a retirement fund on your later years. That is what is called an endowment life insurance. It guarantees a certain amount that you will need on your pre-determined date. Although most of these types of policies are expensive, they will guarantee you the amount stated on the policy whatever the company's investment performance is.

An ordinary life insurance can also be used for this purpose. When the time comes and everything is well set: meaning you don't need financial protection anymore, all your dependents have their own lives already and your estate planning is well taken care of, you can surrender your life insurance policy in return for its cash value and earnings. You can use that money as an additional retirement fund.

But the question now would be: how much retirement fund do I need to prepare? Going back to our previous example, Carlos, let's try to determine how much retirement fund Carlos needs for his retirement. Usually we say that Carlos can retire at the year when his youngest child finishes college. But of course it's up to Carlos to decide when he wants to.

The first question for Carlos is, if he will retire at this point in time how much does he think he will need in order for him to live his life comfortably? Carlos said that he will be needing P20,000 monthly if he will retire today. And we further assumed that he wants to retire at age 56 when his youngest child graduates from college. It means Carlos still has 26 years before his retirement given his current age of 30. With this we need to find out how much would be the future value of P20,000 for his retirement year. We can do that by multiplying P20,000 with the factor of inflation rate (refer to the table on the right).

Years before Retirement	Factor	Years before Retirement	Factor
1	1.06	22	3.60
2	1.12	23	4.82
3	1.19	24	4.05
4	1.26	25	4.29
5	1.34	26	4.55
6	1.42	27	4.82
7	1.50	28	5.11
8	1.59	29	5.42
9	1.69	30	5.74
10	1.79	31	6.09
11	1.90	32	6.45
12	2.01	33	6.84
13	2.13	34	7.25
14	2.26	35	7.69
15	2.40	36	8.15
16	2.54	37	8.64
17	2.69	38	9.15
18	2.85	39	9.70
19	3.03	40	10.29
20	3.21	41	10.90
21	3.40	42	11.56

Table 3.4 Table of Factor of Inflation (based on 6%) for retirement

Given all the assumptions, Carlos will need P21,840,000 for his retirement fund. How did we arrive to that huge amount? Here is how we did it.

P20,000 x 4.55 = P91,000 x 12 = P1,092,000/5% = P21,840,000

You might ask: why that big amount? Lots of retiree who received their retirement benefits made the colossal mistake of spending everything the moment they receive the money. Some of them don't even have the patience to wait that long, so what they usually do is go to lending institutions and borrow money with huge interests, using their retirement benefits as their collateral.

What Carlos should do is re-invest the money that would give him a fixed income as per our assumption 5%. Therefore:

P21,840,000 x 5% = P1,092,000 (annually) or P91,000 (monthly)

With this, even if Carlos lives until the age of 100 he has nothing to worry about for his own money will take care of him. He can enjoy his golden years peacefully without bothering his children. He can even afford to get a special nurse for himself if he needs one to take care of him.

Others would ask, "What would I do with my money if I saved for so long and I'm not going to spend it. Don't I have the right to spend it? Isn't the reason why I save that fund is for me to spend it on my retirement?"

If you can determine the exact date when you are going to die, then you can. But the trick of life is we don't know when our time will come. Just think about this: if you were able to use that fund for, let's say another 40 years and it made your life comfortable, do you think passing it on to your grand children as their inheritance is a bad idea? I'm sure you can let it go the moment you reach that point. After all you can't bring that with you, so why not convert that currency into a currency that heaven recognizes (that is if you believe in heaven): LOVE. You can use it to build love all around you, and even donate it to your chosen charity.

There is another way to prepare for your retirement; it is called the 20/20 rule that says that you need to invest 20 years before your retirement if you want to be in retirement for 20 years.

The question is, do you want to live for only 20 years after your retirement?

I'm sure that at this point, you already recognize how important having life insurance is. So stop thinking that life insurance is about preparing for death, there are a lot more things about it than meets the eye.

If you will notice that most third world countries neglect the issue of life insurance. You can't blame them for their first priority is the food on their table. But what is the chance that you may alleviate poverty if you don't have a saving's leverage?

Like in my case, I came from a poor family. What if I don't get savings leverage, work all my life and spend everything I earn on the things I want today. What if all of a sudden, life plays a trick on me and I become disabled. What is the chance of my family's survival and my dream of financial freedom? Would I have a chance? I don't think so. My children will bear the same poverty that I experienced and if they also don't get saving's leverage then the same fate will happen to them. How can I have my dream of having financial freedom for my family and for the next generation come true? Now you know why most of the poor countries remain poor.

If you think you have money problems today and your income is not enough, then the greater is the need for you to insure your income.

Points to Ponder

> "The only thing money gives you is the freedom
> of not worrying about money.
> ***Johnny Carson***

The basis of your retirement is not your wage but your savings. The moment you reach your required retirement fund you can retire anytime you want. Plan your retirement long before you retire.

The moment you start to accumulate income you should also start setting aside for your retirement. Do you want to know the secret to financial disaster? **Planning your retirement when you're retired.**

Protect your income by having life insurance. When someone is depending on your income, you should ask yourself how you can support them even in your absence. Some are afraid to have life insurance for they think that their spouses would just remarry and others would enjoy the money they had worked hard to save. Fact is; most women remarry after their husbands die not because they want to but because they need someone to help them financially. When you assure your wife that you can still support her and your children even if you leave them unexpectedly, remarrying is just an option.

When you get sick, injured, or are diagnosed with a critical illness; definitely you'll lose your earning ability. Then your family loses income. Though there are four more sources of income for your family—relatives, friends, charity and insurance—which would you prefer?

Consider this, did somebody tell you that "I will take care of your family whenever something happens to you . . ." Yes your relatives could help you but up to what extent? My mother and her siblings learned this the hard way when their father died. All of them were separated from each other, needing to work even at their young age or to be adopted by other relatives in order for them to survive.

Surely you will not bother your friends for they also have their own problems to take care of. Charity can help you but you have to eat your pride and be determined to keep asking help from the PCSO (Philippine Charity Sweepstakes Office] or the charitable foundations of T.V. networks.

Yes, life insurance can't bring your life back, but it has the capability to replace your ability to earn money.

Buying insurance for income protection is like buying peace of mind. Remember that Life Insurance is like renting money at a lower price. If you are living on interest then maybe insurance is just optional to you, like a house: why rent when you can have your own?

CHAPTER 3

THE VEHICLE FOR THE ROAD TO RICHES

Investment is not only volatile; it is the key motor of the economy's prosperity because it has a snowball effect.
Will Hutton
British author and newspaper editor
The State We're In

Investors should remember that excitement and expenses are their enemies. And if they insist on trying to time their participation in equities, they should try to be fearful when others are greedy and greedy when others are fearful
Warren Buffet

How can an ordinary worker or an OFW be financially free? Or perhaps how can even a rich man become richer? The answer is by learning how to ride a vehicle that travels on the road to riches. That is why financial education is so important, it's like taking driving lessons. Everybody says investing is risky but isn't driving risky too? That is why you need to enroll in a driving school. You learn by first trying to drive slowly with a professional driving instructor by your side. Slowly, you then begin to have the courage to try it on your own until eventually driving becomes second nature to you and you would have mastered the fear of driving. The same holds true when it comes to investing.

The reason why people are struggling financially is due to their lack of financial education. Our Filipino culture values education very much. Parents will do everything to make both ends meet just to be able to send their children to school. But the problem is when we go to school we are educated by a system that does not teach us to become financially free but rather to become dependent in working or having a job as a means for a living.

"Study hard, get good grades, so you can apply in a nice company then later on go to America" That is the usual mantra of most parents. I first came to understand this after reading the Robert Kiyosaki's book "Rich Dad, Poor Dad". I'm not going to discuss his "conspiracy of the rich" theory in this book, but I highly recommend his book to all my clients and friends to read it. For me it was a mind opener.

We often ask: why do we struggle financially after attending school? If you have problems understanding money matters, the best way to understand the root of it is by looking at your parents, for they are the ones, who most of the time, teach us about the subject of money. You will say "But my dad did not teach me, in fact he barely talked about it and neither did my mom." Maybe they didn't teach you verbally but the way they handled money matters and money problems at home became your only training when it comes to financial things.

I remember when I first sailed to sea and came back home. I had a lot of money by the end of that contract and it was my first time to handle a huge amount. I then encountered my first dilemma with having so much money. Since my only knowledge about money management was where to spend it, after all, money is used to buy things. As expected, in a few weeks time the money

I saved up from working a year aboard ship was now gone. It was not a good experience for me.

I then promised myself that the next time I come home I'll invest my money. So on my vacation after my second contract, I did not hesitate to invest it. The problem was, I didn't know anything about investments or investment instruments other than a bank so naturally that's where my money went—into the bank. I opened a Time Deposit account, and I said to myself "Wow! I feel so rich!" as it was my first ever, sophisticated investment.

Looking back now, I cannot help but feel naïve because the succeeding earnings which I got from working at sea always went to the banks. It's not bad to put money in the bank, but if your goal is to increase its value over time, banks may not a good place to put it. But at that time my problem was that I knew nothing about other investment vehicles. The very first time I heard of the UITF (Unit Investment Trust Funds) from my friend I thought that it was some kind of sickness related to UTIs (Urinary Tract Infections) It was then that my interest in the world of money matters awakened.

Remember the story of Mike and Myla in the previous chapter? How could Mike have P3,640,421 and Myla with P3,083,646 on their retirement? The answer is by investing their money. If they just kept their P25,000 monthly in their piggy banks, Mike would only have P200,000 while Myla would only have P775,000. Just imagine how big the difference is.

But what is investment anyway? Though saving and investing are usually used interchangeably, these in reality convey entirely two different things. Savings is the amount of money not spent from your income. Whenever you receive your regular income and you set aside a portion of it, that is what you call your savings. You then let it stay in your bank account to earn a small interest. Like when we were young our practice of savings is feeding it to "Oink Oink" or our piggy banks.

Until you take this money out of your savings and ride it into a vehicle or instrument that offers a much desirable return in exchange for its associated risk then it becomes an investment. This means making an active decision to do something productive with your savings by participating in available investment vehicles.

In this chapter we are going to talk about the different investment vehicles available in the market. A long time ago when I was then considered financially illiterate, I didn't understand any of these. But then I came to realize that the only way to achieve wealth is to study wealth, and that is what I'm going to teach you. I will not give you the full intricate details of each investment, for we need to write volumes of books for that, but at least I can give you an over view of what they are.

This will be your starting point in understanding these things that, once upon a time, only bankers, accountants and lawyers understood. But I would highly recommend that you continue studying these different investment vehicles. Just a word of advice that what you don't know you don't touch. Like Mike and Myla you can invest your money in a wide variety of choices of different investment vehicles available in the market that you can feel comfortable with and understand well. So let's discuss them.

MUTUAL FUNDS AND UITF

Whatever method you use to pick stocks of stock mutual funds, your ultimate success or failure will depend on your ability to ignore the worries of the world long enough to allow your investments to succeed. It isn't the head but the stomach that determines the fate of the stock-picker.

Peter Lynch
Investment manager,
Beating the Street

MUTUAL FUNDS

What are Mutual funds? It is an investment that pools the money saved by individuals or even institutions who would want to invest it in various investment vehicles available in the market who share a common investment goal. It simply means that your money together with the money of other investors will be put in one fund. The fund will then be managed by somebody who understands and knows where it will be best invested to let your money grow.

The returns generated by the fund will be distributed amongst the investors depending on the number of shares you have in the fund. Mutual funds are suitable for people who are just beginning to understand the concept of investing for there is somebody called a fund manager, who will take care of your investment. It is also a good vehicle for people who fairly understand the business of investments but don't have the time to take care of it. Since mutual funds provide services for your investment, it charges you a fee. So before you start investing in it you should clearly understand the fees that they charge. Always read the fine print in their prospectus.

Mutual funds offer a wide range of funds to choose from which have specific investment objectives and strategies that match your risk appetite. Investors buy and sell shares of the fund based on the prevailing Net Asset Per Shares (NAVPS) of the day.

To understand more the concept of mutual funds let's compare it with the banks. When you place your money in the bank you are called a depositor or creditor because you lent your money to the bank that in turn guarantees you interest in the money you deposited. The bank will then invest your money in different investment vehicles in the market such as the stock market, government securities, real estate, commercial papers and retail loans. The bank will take all risks associated with these investments and the return it offers. No matter what the bank earns on their investments, you will only receive the guaranteed interest that they promised you.

Referring to Figure 4.1, let's say the bank earns 40% annually, you will only receive what the bank promised you, let say they give a 1% guaranteed interest per annum. Tax will still be deducted from that 1% earning. But, when the bank suffer losses, let's just say-40% per annum you will still receive your guaranteed 1% gross annual interest. The good thing with banks is that they don't usually suffer loss every year or else they would have to shut down their business. Although the past decade we've seen big banks close shop. If for ten consecutive years the bank earns 24% compounded annually on their investment; you as a depositor will still earn only 1% compounded annually. So if you think putting your money in the bank alone will make you realize your financial goals, think again.

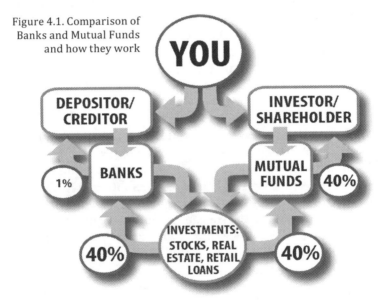

Figure 4.1. Comparison of Banks and Mutual Funds and how they work

On the other hand, if you put your money in mutual funds you are called an investor or a shareholder, meaning you are part owner of the fund depending on the number of shares you have. Then the money pooled by the fund will be invested by the fund manager in different investment vehicles available in the market that the banks also invest in. If the fund earns 40% on their investment, this return will be distributed to all shareholders; but conversely, if the fund suffers loss, this loss will be the investor's loss too.

Sounds scary? Don't be, for when it comes to paper asset investments like stocks, mutual funds and alike, the losses that you see on T.V. every night at business news are just paper losses. And the same thing, if the news says that the stock market or your fund gained so much today, that is just paper gain. What does it mean? Meaning to say, you will only realize your loss or gain the moment you liquidate your investments. Meaning that if on the day you liquidate your investment and the current market price is high, then you gain but if the market price is low then you lose.

The money that you have invested in the fund is not referred to as money anymore but as shares. The number of shares you can have depends on the price per share at the time you invested your money. For you to know the current value of your investment, just multiply the number of your shares with the current NAVPS of the day.

So what do we mean by paper loss and paper gain? For example, if you bought 1,000 shares of a fund at P10 per share, your current account value would be P10,000. After a month you checked the price and you found out that the value per share has decreased to P8. If you multiply your 1,000 shares with P8, your new account value has become P8,000. Does it mean your money looses P2,000? Yes, in paper, and they call it paper loss. It will become a real loss only if you withdraw your investment at the time that it was P8 per share.

Then after another month, you saw that the price per share has increased to P12. If you multiply your 1,000 shares, it will give you a current account value of P12,000. Does it mean your money earned P2,000? Yes, but again in paper and they call it paper gain, but not real gain. It will only be real gain once you encash your shares. But these losses and gains will never be accumulated, that's the usual reaction I get from my clients. The value of your investment is entirely dependent on the current price per share. The good news is, if you just make a good study of investments you will see that over time its value will increase regardless of its everyday fluctuation.

So why do prices of shares of mutual funds fluctuate? Since mutual funds are invested in different varieties of paper assets like stocks, bonds, government securities and real properties, these investments also changes its market price. Therefore the value of your fund will depend on the current performance of where the fund manager invested your money. It will be complicated for you to absorb these fluctuations for now, but the good news is that you don't have to worry about the daily movement of the market for it is the fund manager's job to worry about that.

Here are the other advantages that mutual funds offer that an average investor may not be able to enjoy if he or she invests directly in the market.

Professionally Managed

As what we have learned, investing needs to be studied. Mutual funds employ highly experienced professionals that do investments on a full-time basis and we call them fund managers. They also have teams of experts in computer and accounting systems to do extensive research in able to manage investors' money that matches the fund's objectives.

But it also means that you have no or little control on your own investment for they are the ones who will decide when and where to put your money and in what company to invest in. Whatever the results of their investment decisions will be, the fund holder of a particular mutual fund will bear the consequences. That's why it is important that you need to choose carefully the mutual fund company that you will be investing with. Review their past performances, although past performances do not guarantee future returns but it will give you a historical overview on how they managed their investor's money.

It's also good to do a comparative of each mutual fund company. You can visit the website of Investment Company Association of the Philippines (www.icap.com.ph), where they list the daily as well as the historical performance of each fund of all mutual fund companies available in the Philippines.

Liquidity

Your money in mutual funds is highly liquid. Liquidity means the availability to readily convert investments into cash. Investments such as real estate are not considered liquid because supposing you suddenly need money badly, for example for hospital bills, you cannot make instant money out of your investment; you have to find a buyer for you to enable to convert it into cash and this process takes time. Such is not the case with mutual funds for the fund itself will buy back your shares whenever you need to liquidate your investment basing it on the prevailing Net Asset Value Per Shares or NAVPS. However, each mutual fund has its own holding period for its individual funds. If you withdraw your investment within the holding period, a corresponding fee is deducted.

Diversification

When it comes to investments, there is no such thing as a sure thing. This is the reason why you have to diversify your investments into different asset classes. So that in case one of your investments does not perform well or worse, crashes, hopefully the others will do well or better. The problem is when you only have a limited amount of money, diversification can be hard to do. In mutual funds, since it is pooling investors' money, the amount of money available for investment becomes greater and it enables the fund to spread it in various securities resulting in a greater inclination to earn more. Not only is the money well diversified, even the risks can be spread across the different investment vehicles.

For example, you have money in the bank in the amount of P20,000. You then decided to transfer your investment into the stock market to take advantage of much greater earnings. Then you decided to invest it in PLDT, where the minimum number of shares that you can buy is 5 shares. If the price per share of PLDT is P2,400, you can buy 8.3 shares. However, there is a minimum number of shares you have to buy called the board lot (1 board lot in PLDT is 5 shares], your money can therefore buy only 1 board lot which will cost you P12,000. It means your P20,000 can buy only

1 board lot since the P8,000 excess is not enough to buy another board lot of PLDT.

With mutual funds your P20,000 will go to the pool of money together with the other investors of that particular fund. With that, the fund can now buy not only shares of PLDT but shares in other companies as well as that the fund manager decided, and the fund can be invested not only in stocks but in bonds as well.

Low Capital Requirement

Starting an investment in mutual funds requires only a minimum of P5,000 initial investment and P1,000 for subsequent investments. Unlike if you are going to invest directly in the stock market or in government securities, it will usually require a substantial capital to invest in a diversified portfolio. With this, there is no more reason for you not to start your own investment. Remember it's not how big but how regular you do your investment.

Tax Free

At the time of writing of this book, earnings from mutual funds are one of the items excluded from items classified as taxable income. This is a provision of R.A. 8424 or the Comprehensive Tax Reform Package (CTRP) of 1998. In comparison, the interest that we receive from our peso savings accounts and time deposits are subject to a 20% tax while for foreign currencies, they are subject to a 7.5% final withholding tax.

UITFs or UNIT INVESTMENT TRUST FUNDS

What are UITFs? After discussing what mutual funds are, it will now be easier for you to understand the UITF or Unit Investment Trust Funds for it is very similar to mutual funds. It is a "trust" product, meaning you are entrusting your money to the company offering the UITF, called the "trustee". In mutual funds you are a shareholder (technically you have a "share" or a part of the company where you have investments in] of but in UITFs you are not part owner of the company but you are a "trustor".

UITFs are offered by banks. When you place your money in that fund, you don't own a part of the bank but instead you just entrust your money with their Trust Group. But your money is not treated like an ordinary deposit, it is not covered by the PDIC Insurance (Philippine Deposit Insurance Corp.] meaning that just like in mutual funds, the loss of capital is possible. The table below is to summarize the difference between Mutual Funds and UITFs.

FEATURE	MUTUAL FUNDS	UITF
Offered By	Investment Company	Banks
Manages the fund's assets	Employed by the company	Trust Group of the Bank
Structure	Corporate	Contractual
Sale Agents	CIS Licensed	No license required
Pricing	NAVPS (Net Asset Value Per Share]	NAVPU (Net Asset Value Per Unit]
Investor Status	Shareholders	Trustor
Applicable Fee	Entry Fee, Exit Fee	Trust Fee
Regulating Body	Securities and Exchange Commission	Banko Sentral ng Pilipinas
Protecion by Law	"Investment Company Act of the Philippines"	No specific law is applicable, though banks are governed by the "General Banking Law"

Table 4.1 Difference between Mutual funds and UITF

An investment company offers various fund types which are categorized according to their investment objectives or the instruments that they are primarily invested in. Before you invest in any fund, make sure that the one you choose should be according to your investment attitude.

Remember that investing is like a roller coaster ride, there are ups and downs along the way and it's a good thing that while these things happen, you can still have a good night's sleep while enjoying the journey. It also depends on the currency that you have available for investing, for OFWs, investing in dollars may be suitable. But investing in foreign currency poses an additional risk—currency risk. Even if your investment in foreign currency appreciates in value, if the exchange rate of that currency versus peso drops; then maybe you don't gain at all or worse the real value of your money in peso drops.

In the Philippines, Funds are categorized into four types:

Equity/Stock Fund-A type of fund primarily invested in the stock market listed at the Philippine Stock Exchange [PSE]. This is ideal for somebody who wants to take part of the growth of a growing public corporation but does not have the expertise nor the time to manage his or her investments. This is suitable for the investor who can take a higher risk tolerance in exchange for a much higher return. Though it is primarily invested in the stock market, some companies allocate a small portion of their fund in cash or fixed-income instrument to protect the fund during a stock market decline.

Balance Fund-A fund which investment strategy is a combination of stocks and fixed-income instruments which gives a 50/50 allocation for both, hence it was called balance fund. Depending on the market outlook and projection of the fund manager, this 50/50 strategy is constantly adjusted to make the fund gain a higher return but maintain its balance as much as possible. This fund is suitable for investors who want a significant amount of income but are mindful of market volatility. If you can tolerate a medium risk, this fund is for you.

Bond Fund-A fund which gives a much higher earning in comparison to savings products. This is ideal for the risk-averse investor who wants to save to at least beat inflation. Why is it ideal to a risk-averse person? For the reason that the majority of its fund is allocated in government securities like bonds. Government bonds is almost a risk free investment. What is bond? Bond in simple terms means debt. Government issues bonds and sells it to fund their projects and other financial needs to run our government. We will discuss more about this in the succeeding chapters.

However, bond funds are not totally risk free because a portion of it is invested in corporate bonds—debt instruments issued by private corporations. Since they are private companies, there is a chance that these companies might go bankrupt, with that they offer a much higher interest compared with government bonds. Unlike corporate bonds, the government will simply print money to pay for their debts.

Money Market Funds-Money Market is a debt instrument which matures in less than one year. It includes T-bills, as well as other long term debt instruments like all types of bonds and Treasury Notes. Money market fund is ideal for conservative investor for it is very liquid and relatively safe. This fund protects your capital while giving modest returns.

Remember, investing in mutual funds and UITFs means entrusting your hard earned money to other people to do the investing decisions. The question remains, should we invest directly in the stock market or we should just get a mutual fund? Well, if you really want to select your own stock portfolio then you must o it yourself—invest directly in the stock market and get a broker to assist you. If you think you can really trust your broker then combining your knowledge and his advice might do it for you. But be wary for there are brokers whose least concern is their client's welfare. Brokers make money on every transaction they make, whether you gain or lose, your broker will still get his commission. An antagonist once said: "That's why they are called brokers—to make you broke". But if you don't want to listen to your broker then you can do your own research, start reading business news or subscribe to various business newsletters available specially on the internet. Then instead of getting a broker you can invest in the stock market via an online brokerage that charges a relatively much lower commission. Continuous education like reading books and attending seminars will dramatically improve your investing attitude and knowledge.

But what is the major advantage of investing in mutual funds and UITFs compared with direct investing in stock market? Let's say you want to build your house and you are not an architect or engineer. And your budget for your dream house is P10 million pesos. Are you going to risk building it yourself or are you going to hire somebody to do it for you, someone who you know has more professional knowledge than you. That somebody has spent more than 4 years in college and has a range of experience on the house building business. I'm sure you're not going to gamble your P10 million budget for your house by building it yourself that you know honestly you have no idea about. But still, most novice investors take that risk and let their ego and pride drive them down the ditch and after losing their millions that's the only time they will evaluate what they have done.

Yes it is costly to hire them, but just think of the convenience and comfort it would give you. You can continue doing your own day time job and errands that make you busy while somebody is making your money multiply. But the same way in choosing your architect or engineer, you have to check the performance of the company that you would want to handle your money, although past performance is not always an indication of future return.

Does it mean that you should not invest by yourself in the stock market? I am not saying that, it's just a matter of how much time and effort you can devote by studying and doing research to become as good as the architect or engineer in our analogy.

Everybody wants to be rich but the problem is only a few want to work for it. There is no better investment that you can start than self investment—invest in your personal education so you can be as good as or much better than any fund manager out there. Being rich is lifelong commitment; remember there is no short cut to success.

SECURITIES

Bull markets are born on pessimism; grow on skepticism,
mature on optimism, and die on euphoria.

Michael B. Steele

After learning investing in mutual funds let's now proceed to a much advanced vehicle—the stock market. If you started with mutual funds, at least you will now feel how it is to be an investor. We often hear the word investment and speculation in the financial world, but what is the difference between the two? There is a wide debate on defining these words depending on the person's formula to make their money multiply.

Some say that speculation is a risky assumption that your money will earn in a short term period; while investing is putting your money in long term and hoping for a good return. Wait a second, it looks the same to me—an assumption for gain in a short term period and hoping for a long term return. In both cases you are speculating. I think it is much safer to say that speculation is failure investment due to a lack of analysis and investment is a successful, calculated speculation. With this I will not discuss speculation because I do not recommend for you to fail in your investment—I think that is crazy.

Some people find investing in the stock market a very exciting task while others find it very intimidating. There are people who spend a lot of time reading market reports, watching business news, or checking the latest announcements of the prospective company that they are planning to invest in. While for some, putting their money in the stock market would be the last thing on their minds.

Somebody asked me, "When is the best time to join the Market?" To which I replied "Every day is the best time.", provided that you have taken care of the basic things first, it applies not only in stock market investing but for any type of investment venture. Zero in on your bad debts first, take control of your credit card and make sure you can keep up with the mortgages for your house and car. Remember, the return in your investment will not give you an immediate result but the interest payment due on your debts is a sure thing; worst it will multiply faster than your investment. Don't forget too, to build your back-up fund (3 to 6 times of your monthly expenses] first, to make sure you have a back up for any untoward event like losing your job. The personal element is the larger or lesser significant factor in any investment decision you'll make.

INVESTMENT PORTFOLIO MANAGEMENT

In the last twenty years, the right course was to be disciplined and steady. In the next ten years, be firm in the conviction that you will only know a few things; they will change and be short term.
The goal is real absolute terms, not relative performance.

Dean LeBaron,
quoted in Five
Eminent Contrarians,
by Steven L. Mintz,
1994

A portfolio is a list of combinations of different assets or classes of investments that matches the purpose of the investor to achieve his or her goals. It may be composed of shares of stocks in the open market, shares of funds in mutual funds, bonds, commodities, arts and even real estate properties, etc. Managing your portfolio means allocating your money into different asset classes available in the market. The fundamental principle of asset allocation is that the older you become the less risk you can take on your investments. And once you retire, your investments should be more conservative, of which a majority of it can be placed in vehicles that will give you a fixed income for the rest of your retirement days. Although that is not an absolute rule, for even if you are a retiree, you can still enjoy investing in stocks. The same thing applies even if you are still in your mid 20's, wherein maybe you would prefer to invest in bonds or fixed income securities. That is why planning and determining the proper proportion of your portfolio is extremely important.

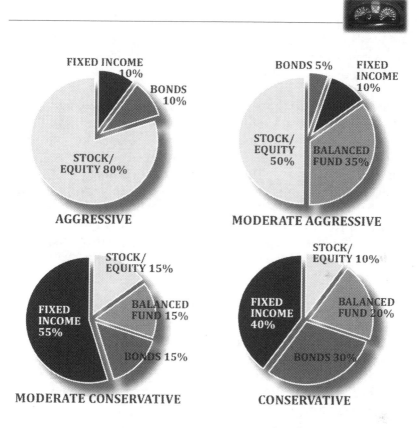

FIXED INCOME 10%

BONDS 10%

STOCK/ EQUITY 80%

AGGRESSIVE

BONDS 5%

FIXED INCOME 10%

STOCK/ EQUITY 50%

BALANCED FUND 35%

MODERATE AGGRESSIVE

STOCK/ EQUITY 15%

FIXED INCOME 55%

BALANCED FUND 15%

BONDS 15%

MODERATE CONSERVATIVE

STOCK/ EQUITY 10%

FIXED INCOME 40%

BALANCED FUND 20%

BONDS 30%

CONSERVATIVE

Figure 4.2. Four types of Investment Allocation

For instance take the case of Jose, a 25 year old, employee. He started investing right after he got his first job. At the beginning, he can be an aggressive investor but once Jose nears his retirement, he must slow down and change his asset allocation and move it to bonds and be a moderate investor.

Another strategy in managing portfolios is market timing. If you can anticipate that the performance of equity for the coming year will not give you a promising yield, then putting it into bonds will at least prevent huge losses on your portfolio. But you should never let your fear decide your investment portfolio; fear is driven by lack of knowledge in what you are doing.

When it comes to investment, there are three characters of people in this world. Who are you among these three?

Bonifacio M. Atapang-A type of investor who is willing to take any risk for a higher return for whatever it will cost, even if he loses a major part of his money. We call this type of investor a High-Risk Investor. This is someone who can sleep well at night without worrying even if the value of his investment portfolio is losing about a quarter in a year. Being a high risk investor is not easy because you have to do a lot of research and study, not to mention the time it will require from you. It is very important for you to have plenty of active advisers if you believe in making quick money in a short period of time. Being plain stupid is very different from being high risk.

Jose M. Edium-Is an investor who wants a capital appreciation on his investment with an average risk exposure. We call this type of person as a Moderate-Risk Investor. His investment portfolio is almost equally divided between equities and bonds. One should realize that as a moderate-risk investor you should have a long term horizon on your investment goals to make your money create more wealth for you.

Armida Sy Gurista-Is a wealth preserver type of person who invests her money by looking for marginal returns over and just above inflation. We call this type of person as a Conservative Investor. Persons like Armida Sy Gurista want investments that are dependable and doesn't want surprises that they would have to worry about. They don't want to risk their capital on mere chance, even at the risk of losing the possibility of gaining high returns on their investments, as long as they will have their money when they need it. Especially if you are already enjoying your retirement, why worry about money, let your money worry for you.

Were you able to find your investing personality after knowing these persons? Another thing to consider in choosing what personality you want to be is your timetable. Even if you are a type of person who is willing to take high-risk investments but just have ten or five years left to retire, it is wiser if you invest conservatively. Inversely the same thing is true when you are just starting to build wealth and still have a lot of time before retirement. It would be wiser if you put your money into something that will give more growth opportunities. Even if you lose part of it there will still be a lot of time for you to recover.

One thing however, whether you are Bonifacio, Jose or even Armida; you must know what you are doing. Don't invest into something just because you received a hot tip about a new investment opportunity. Though, every investment involves a certain level of risk. Whether you risk losing part of your money for a much higher return or risk losing a chance to earn greater returns in choosing to preserve your capital. However, not investing at all is the most risky thing of all. It is your hard earned money, I will say it again, invest heavily first on your financial education. What you don't know, you don't touch.

When it comes to investing, the biggest dilemma for us is where to put our money. Like myself in the beginning, when I did not understand anything about investing, my only option was to put my money in the bank. A lack of financial education will give us very limited options in increasing our wealth.

When ordinary people think about growing their wealth, putting up a business is the first thing that usually comes to their mind. There is nothing wrong about that, in fact that's one of the fastest ways but when you ask them what kind of business, immediately they will tell you they'd want to put up a sari-sari store (small community retail store]. What's wrong with that, you might ask? Nothing, it's a good starting point and I don't demean putting up a sari-sari store.

But do you know one sari-sari store that became a grocery or even supermarket? Maybe groceries that became a sari-sari store—yes, there is a lot of that—after losing their business.

The sari-sari store is a good business idea, but the problem is that the sari-sari store mentality that we Filipinos have, is to just to put up a business with the main goal of sustaining our everyday needs. We do not even monitor what is going on with our sales. We usually take all our daily needs from that business, even payment for our electric and other utility bills.

If you are really serious with putting up a sari-sari store or retailing business, I suggest that you at least study basic business recording, to understand what is going with in your business.

Aside from putting your money in a business, there are other asset classes where you can invest your money. As we talk about assets, there are four primary asset classes:

First is business; it means you become an entrepreneur: putting up a sari-sari store, buy and sell, having a bakery or other similar businesses. We usually call it a traditional business, having a physical business that you run. Second is real estate—investing in raw land, buildings or rental properties. Third is paper assets—mutual funds, stocks, bond or bank deposits. Fourth is commodities—gold, silver, oil, gas, rare metals.

In this chapter, we are about to discuss the third type of asset—paper assets. On a previous section we have talked about Mutual Funds and UITFs. Now we are going to talk about Stocks and Bond.

So what is the stock market? It is an organized market that encompasses the buying and selling (exchange] of securities (stocks and bonds]. In the Philippines, the PSE (Philippine Stock Exchange] is the only operating stock exchange with two trading floors: one in the PSE Plaza in Ayala, Makati City and the other in the PSE Center in Ortigas, Pasig City. At present, its daily sessions are from 9am to 12nn and 1pm to 3pm except Saturdays, Sundays, legal holidays and days when the BSP (Banko Sentral ng Pilipinas] clearing office is closed.

To understand clearly the difference between stocks and bonds, let's put it in one scenario. Steve wants to start a garment business. After making a careful study he found out that he will be needing P500,000 as a starting capital. But Steve only has P250,000 in savings, so he is short of another P250,000.

In order for him to pursue his business, he can go to the bank and take out a loan for additional capital. But he realized that once he takes a loan from the bank, he would need to pay monthly for the principal of the loan plus its interest. He knows that it will cost him so much and would be difficult for a business man like him who is just starting up.

The bank is not the only source of capital funding for Steve. He can invite his friends to join him in his business or he can take out a loan from his friend instead of getting it from the bank.

Let's say Steve decides to invite his five friends and asks each of them P50,000 to invest in his business. If his five friends invest P50,000 each, they would then become part owner of his business, each owning ten percent of the business including all equipment and other assets as well as ten percent of all earnings of the business in the future. That is how stock investment works.

But how about if Steve issues a loan certificate? Instead of asking them to be his partner, he will sell these certificates to his five friends for P50,000 each with an interest of 7% every year for five years. This time he is not looking for a partnership but rather a loan. His five friends will not become owner of Steve's business, but rather be like the bank—Steve will owe them money. The advantage of this is that Steve doesn't need to pay every month for the capital of the loan. He only needs to pay the interest until the maturity of the loan. It would be much easy for Steve for he only needs to worry about the interest payments until he can recover all his capital from the earnings of his business. At the end of the loan agreement, Steve hopes that he will have enough funds to pay for his loan. And above all, he still has 100% ownership of his business. That is how bond investment works.

So the question now is, would you like to be a partner in business of a corporation or you just want them to lend money? With this, we can discuss deeper each of these Securities—bonds and stocks.

STOCK SECURITIES

One of the funny things about the stock market is that every time one man buys, another sells, and both think they are astute.
William Feather

Let's talk about Stock Securities. It is a share of ownership in a corporation depending on how many shares you bought. As owner of stock—or stockholder, you have a claim on the company's assets as well as on its earnings.

Suppose I want to start a food factory and I will need 1 million pesos to start my business and I don't want to borrow from the bank. So instead, I decide to use my P100,000 savings in the bank. Since I need another P900,000 to complete my needed capital, I invite nine of my high school friends to join me in the business and each of them agree to put in P100,000 also. In return for their P100,000 investment, I will give them a certificate which represents ten percent ownership of my company, including the plants, equipment and other assets of my company. Their certificates also represent ten percent of the future earnings of my company.

After a couple of years, the total value of my company becomes two million. This means that each of our share has grown from P100,000 to P200,000—which is twice our initial investment.

Now, my nine friends have the option to keep their share or sell it to other interested investors for P200,000. That is 100% profit for my friends. That looks good, but if my business did not perform as expected, whatever loss I will incur would be their loss too.

Shares of stock can be purchased either through an IPO (Initial Public Offering] or through the open market. You can have a share of stock of one corporation thru their IPO which will be sold to the primary market. This is the first time that the company will offer their shares to the public. The proceeds of the IPO will go directly to the company for them to finance their needed additional capitalization.

I can almost hear you say, "Wait, what are these IPO, primary market and secondary market thing?"

To understand this clearly, let me put it this way: suppose you want to buy a brand new car. So you went to your selected car manufacturer or dealer. You choose the type and model of car you want and pay the manufacturer of the car through your agent. Then after 1 year of driving your car, you plan to sell it so you can buy a newer car. So you look for a buyer and you land an easy deal and sell it. By this time, the proceeds of the sales will no longer go to the car manufacturer but to you who is the rightful owner of that car.

That is similar to an IPO when the corporation sells its shares for the first time. The proceeds of the sales will naturally go to the corporation. That type of transaction is called the primary market. Since you now have ownership of a certain amount of shares, you have the legal right to hold it for as long as you want or sell it to another person. And once you sell it to another person, the proceeds will no longer go to the corporation but to you. That transaction is called secondary market selling.

People usually interchange the word stock with the phrase common stock. There are two main categories of stocks; common stocks and preferred stocks and the benefits and rights vary between these two.

Preferred Stocks take priority over the common stock. Meaning once the corporation goes bankrupt and their assets get liquidated, preferred stock holders will receive a share of the proceeds before common stockholders. Usually preferred stock holders are entitled to receive a fixed dividend before any payments of dividend is made to common stock holders. Technically, this share is bought for fixed income and safety of principal.

Common Stock holders are junior or secondary to preferred stockholders. It simply means that when the company earns they are not the first priority to receive dividends, rather the preferred stockholders. That's the reason why preferred stocks are called senior. Same thing when the company goes bankrupt, preferred stockholders receive payments first. Then whatever is left will be divided among the common stockholders.

Since dividends and equity do not have fixed value for common stocks unlike preferred stocks, they now have a greater chance of earning when the company performs well and inversely, when the company is doing poorly, they will suffer most. It means that common stock is more risky compared to preferred stock.

Investors gain profits in the stock market thru capital gain—when the market price of stocks increases compared to the price when you bought it, or thru cash dividends—when the company returns part of its earning to their investors.

Somebody asked me, "How can I invest in the stock market if I don't have a million pesos in my pocket?" Well, that's why you have to invest in the stock market, to put millions in your pocket. Don't follow other people who have lost millions from their pocket by investing in the market. The stock market is not a big casino where you gamble your money away. On the other hand, there is no need to panic because today, for as low as P5,000 you can now start investing in the stock market.

PRICE RANGE	TICK SIZE	BOARD LOT
0.0001 to 0.0099	0.0001	1,000,000
0.01 to 0.049	0.001	100,000
0.05 to 0.249	0.001	10,000
0.25 to 0.495	0.005	10,000
0.5 to 4.99	0.01	1,000
5 to 9.99	0.01	100
10 to 19.98	0.02	100
20 to 49.95	0.05	100
50 to 99.95	0.05	100
100 to 199.9	0.10	10
200 to 499.8	0.20	10
500 to 999.5	0.50	10
1000 to 1999	1.00	5
2000 to 4998	2.00	5
5000 & above	5.00	5

Table 4.2 Board Lot and Fluctuation Table

Take for example the case of Agnes, after learning of the investment opportunities in the stock market; she decided to be a shareholder of SM. After losing a lot of her hard earned money by being a frequent shopper of SM, she decided to capture back her losses by being a business partner of Herny Sy, and that is by purchasing shares of stocks of SM. Now isn't it a good idea?

Shares of stock are usually sold in groups of 100, which are called round lots and in groups of less than 100 which are termed odd lots. Board lots of stock market varies and it depends on the market price of the stock and its price fluctuation.

If Agnes decided to buy 100 shares of stocks of SM and for example SM has a million shares of outstanding stock, it means Agnes has one-thousandth share of SM. Even if Agnes doesn't have that much money to start with and she decides to buy only 10 shares, as long as SM makes a profit, she is entitled to their shares and benefits.

The table below shows the charges and taxes levied on the investors which is subject to change but at the time of this writing, is still applicable:

Fees/Taxes	Seller	Buyer
1. Brokerage commission (max 1.5% of transaction cost + 12% VAT	Yes	Yes
2. SCCP fee of 0.0001 x value of transaction	Yes	Yes
3. Transfer fee of P 100.00 + 12% VAT	Yes	Yes
4. Cancellation fee of P 20.00 + VAT%	Yes	Yes
5. Stock Transaction Tax (1/2 of 1% value of ytansaction in lieu of capital gain tax)	Yes	Yes

Going back to Agnes, if she bought SM (Stock Symbol SMPH) at the price of P11.92, using the board lot table, the minimum number of shares she can buy is 100 shares.

Market Price/Share	P	11.92
Min. lot	x	100.00
	= P	1,192.00
Broker's Commision (1.5% + 12% VAT)	+ P	20.02
Transfer Fee + 12% VAT	+ P	112.00
SCCP	+	1.32
Total Cash Needed	P	1,325.34

Imagine, just by having P1,325.34 you can now be part owner of SM, but of course you would still need at least P5,000 to start investing in the stock market. If you want more value for your investment you can do it by minimizing your costs. The only way you can do that is by bypassing a stock broker and doing your own stock trading online. Usually if you don't have at least a million pesos with you, most brokers will just snub you. Although you have to remember that online trading means going it on your own. However, there are some online brokerages that offer some advice thru their research and studies so it would be up to you to study it and take time to read their research or at least attend the free seminars that they usually give.

Think about it, how many P1,000 pesos have you already spent in SM (or in other malls] in the past that you have never recovered? So do you still think that investing in the stock market is risky or is it much riskier spending your money for nothing? How would you feel the next time you attend your high school class reunion and everybody is bragging about their achievements and when it's your turn to brag just say "I'm a business partner of Henry Sy!"

I'm sure the question now in your mind is how do I choose a company to invest with? That's an important question to ask because this will lead to your success or failure in stock investing. The concept on why we are investing in the stock market is based on four promises that they are offering:

- That the company has a good record and has shown an up-trend of earnings and stability on their management.
- That the company has a consistent record of dividend returns to their investors and has good projections that it will still continue to earn.
- That there are enough assets to liquidate in case the company goes bankrupt.
- That in case you need to take control of the company, ask yourself: would this be the kind of company you really want to own?

Where can you get the information you need for analyzing your investment? The terms for respective stock issues are set forth in the charter or articles of incorporation. These are not readily available but once the company gets listed, the most significant provisions in the listing application are obtainable. Another good source of information are the stockholders and annual reports which can be found on the company's website or in the brokerage houses. Some companies even issue monthly, quarterly and semiannual reports.

Surely all those who invest in the stock market are earnings-driven. To fulfill this, first find the best performing industry: communications, banks and financials, commercial and industrial, conglomerates, consumer, properties, services or mining. Then find the best company that belongs to the industry you want to invest in and buy their stocks.

If you do your homework well enough, you will occasionally find research on a particular company that will show that everything looks good on their financial statement and projection, even though they are not the favorite stock of the investing public at the moment. Compare it side by side with other companies of the same industry and do a comparative analysis. After you have no doubt that it's the best pick, then grab that before it takes off, sure enough you have found your gem. Stay away from companies that are unfamiliar to you and will continue to be unfamiliar to you.

Some say that the best way to become an instant millionaire in the stock market is by buying low and selling high, known as market timing. If you really have that expertise or if a fortune teller will be generous enough to lend you her crystal ball then lucky for you. But if that is not the case, do not try it, that's speculation and you will lose your money in the long run.

One time, I attended a training on stock technical analysis and one thing I noticed with most of the participants is that; unlike me they were not new in the stock market. At that time I hadn't started investing yet. When I asked them how much they have gained in their investments, most of them said that they were not investors but that they were traders (they buy when they think the stock is low and sell once the price peaks]. Most of them have lost a huge sum of money. In fact one of them already lost more than a million pesos. And for that reason they were attended that training.

When I asked them their reason for choosing a particular stock, most of them just relied on what they see on the chart without even knowing the nature of the business of that corporation. Another problem with the buy low sell high approach is that it doesn't tell you why the price gets high and why it falls.

Another thing to consider in buying a stock is of course the price, which is a major issue. How would you know if you are buying cheap or expensive shares? Not because stock A is selling at P1.35 per share and stock B is selling a share for P300.00 will mean that stock A is cheaper. There are two prices to consider— the market price and intrinsic value (fair value].

Market price is the price dictated by the general investing public, once that stock becomes famous and attractive, naturally its price will increase. It is governed by the law of supply and demand. But it doesn't mean that the price is equivalent to the real value of the corporation.

Intrinsic value is the real value of the corporation based on their financial statement and earnings. They even include future projections of the company into consideration.

Market price is the price of the stock that you will see when you watch business news or read a newspaper that gives a list of daily stock closing prices.

Intrinsic value can be obtained by doing your home work: reading the financial statements and financial review of that particular corporation.

For example take two companies of the same industry. Stock A is selling in the market for P10 per share and Stock B is P50 per share. Which of them is expensive? If you will rely on market price you will immediately say that it is Stock B. After careful study of their respective financial statements, you find out that Stock A's intrinsic value or fair value is P8 per share while Stock B is P75 per share.

This means that Stock A is way more expensive than Stock B, because you are paying P10 per share where in fact its real value is only P8 per share while Stock B is a value company because you are only paying P50 per share for its P75 worth, which gives you 50% more value on your investment.

While there are different styles in investing strategies, two styles dominate the field which are being practiced. These are Growth Investing Strategy and Value Investing Strategy.

Growth investors generally seek corporations or industries that show strong and sustained growth in their sales and earnings as well as on its trend. If you are this type of investor, you must look for a fast growing company and not sleeping companies in their industry. Usually a growing company sells at a high price so you always have to be on the lookout because if something goes wrong, your portfolio will surely suffer. Even a simple announcement from that company will make the price move either up or down. It's also good to know the people behind that company; their leadership and the way they manage the company will make a lot of difference.

On the other hand, the value investing strategy normally seeks for a high fair value or intrinsic value of the stock that is trading at a low price compared to its book value. But remember this, not because this stock has a high book value and low price will it mean that it will give you a return.

Look at its value as well as its future too. The story of that company or what we called catalysts is very important for that will make the price of its share move. You can also look for corporations whose stocks have fallen during times of recession and was forgotten by the investing public, but shows a very promising future. Being a value investor takes a lot of patience.

So, which style is the best style? That's the million dollar question. Of course growth investing might provide you in the quickest time the higher return than value investing. But that growth being outperformed by its value is the risk associated with growth investing. But if you will just be patient, value investing will surely give you a positive earning and sometimes outperforms the growth investing method.

The next issue now is when do you sell your shares. Most investors find this more difficult than deciding what to buy. Usually this is the time that investors get a flood of emotions.

The main reason why you should say goodbye to your stock is when there is a concern that leads to earnings disappointments. Another is when a stock gets too famous and overvalued that the price to earnings ratio is not reasonable anymore. It is best to sell into buying rage, take your profit and come back later. Warren Buffet said it best, "Be fearful when others are greedy and greedy when others are fearful." If the industry where your stocks belong start to get weak, it tells you that something is going wrong or when criticism of that industry is politically motivated, then selling would be a wise move.

Selling requires great discipline. Another consideration on when to sell is when the behavior of your stock is no longer according to your investment objective. It means that if you are a growth investor and your stocks are acting like value and your value investments acting like growth, then maybe that's the time to part ways from your stocks. Remember this, not every day is a day of celebration there are times that you must be brave enough and admit to yourself that there are times when you not only gain some but also lose some. When that time comes, be mature enough to acknowledge that you have made some mistakes and you've learned from it. Learn to let go when it is time to let go.

STOCK INVESTORS' VOCABULARY

Bull Market: A stock market condition in which prices are rising and it's expected to continue to rise.

Bear Market: The opposite condition of bull market wherein prices of the stocks or commodities are in a falling trend.

Index: The benchmark of the stock market. It is the average movement of shares of stock, it maybe up or down. It doesn't mean that every share went up or down but it means that most stocks move up or down. You may compare it with a batch of students when you say "This school year we have a good batch of students."-it doesn't mean that every student is good but on the average. In the Philippines we called our index as the Phisix, which is composed of 30 companies listed in the market.

Basis Point: It is the difference in yield which is equivalent to 1/100th of a percent (0.01%). 100 basis points are equal to 1.0%. Hence, if previous performance is 30.5% and today is 31.0% market is up by 50 basis points.

Efficient Market Theory: The theory which holds that stocks are always correctly priced since everything that is publicly known about the stock is reflected in its market price.

Random Walk Theory: The opinion that stock price variations are not predictable.

Volume: Refers to the volume of share traded in a day. It is a key way to measure the supply and demand, and is often the primary indicator of new prices. Many investors look at the volume traded on a day in comparison with the average daily volume. When a major event happens whether good or bad or even a major announcement made by companies, stocks can trade ten times its average daily volume.

Peso Cost Averaging: Investing in the market on a regular basis (monthly or quarterly etc.] without considering the market price, even if it goes down or up, for in the long run it will average the cost. It will require good fundamental studies on the company you want to invest with. It is an investment strategy based on random walk theory that you cannot predict when the market price will go down or up.

Technical Analysis: Is the study of stock price movements using the chart to predict the future price movement.

Fundamental Analysis: A study of price movements based on past price and volume movements. Persons investing using this technique often refer to it as chartist for they employ certain patterns from the chart in predicting price movement.

Ask price: Price in which owner of stocks are selling for. **Bid price:** Price in which stock buyer are willing to pay. **Spread:** The difference between the bid and the ask price

DEBT SECURITIES

Investing in bonds requires attention to more than one event at a time. Driving a car requires a foot on the gas, hands on the wheel, and eyes on the road. Navigating the bond market requires a foot on interest rates, a handle on the prospects of being repaid, and an eye on inflation.

Steven Mintz,
Financial journalist
The Art of Investing

After discussing stocks, let's now talk about bonds. A bond is a debt instrument issued by the government, private corporations and other entities in order to finance their projects or activities. In its most fundamental nature, a bond is a loan that investors make to the entities that issues it.

When a company wants to expand, it will require additional capitalization. Aside from selling stocks, issuing bonds will help them to raise the needed funds. As we have discussed ealier, a bond is an evidence of indebtedness. When you buy bonds of a particular corporation, you are lending them your money in return for an agreed interest. Unlike stocks, what you are buying is a position of ownership.

The price of the bond is basically the amount of money that is being loaned, we call that face value. In exchange for this loan the investor receives interest known as a bond coupon; which is usually paid semi-annual or quarterly. It is issued for a specified time such as 1-year, 3-year, 5-year or even more than 10 years.

After the end of this period; the bond matures and the bond issuer repays the loan to the investors at its face value in full.

Bonds are the most senior of all securities issued by a company. With that, most people assume that this is the safest investment. Senior in a way, that when a corporation declares insolvency or bankruptcy, their entire asset will be liquidated to pay off their liabilities and debt. If it happens and you are one of their lenders or you are a bond holder, you will be paid first above those who have stock certificates.

Whatever money is left after paying all liabilities and bond holders, the next one to be paid are the preferred stockholders, and everything that is left will be divided between all common stock holders. So theoretically bond securities are the safest of them all, while common stock securities are the riskiest. Meaning, a common stockholder could earn more or less depending on the asset of the company.

Most novices in bonds are surprised to learn that bond prices change every day. They buy this paper asset and hold on to it until maturity; though it is proper but whenever you see an opportunity you can trade your bond just like you trade your stocks.

How does bonds work? To understand it better, let us take a simple analogy. As in our previous example; I decided to expand my food factory by branching out to other provinces. Instead of going to the bank, I decide to issue bonds for sale to the investing public.

Malou bought one of my bonds issued with a face value of P1,000 and a coupon or interest of 6% with five years maturity. This means that Malou will receive P60 or 6% every year for the next five years. When the bonds mature at the end of five years, I have to return Malou's P1,000 investment.

As I have said, just like with stocks, bonds can be traded; it means that Malou can also sell her bond before it matures.

The reason why corporations issue bonds is to finance their current capital project, like expanding a business, buying new equipment or financing their new buildings while governments issue bonds to finance infrastructure projects and construction, as well as for other social services.

Technically speaking a bond refers to a debt instrument which has a maturity of ten years or more. But most people use this term for almost any debt instrument regardless of maturity. Bills are a fix instrument which matures in a year or less for example Treasury Bills or T-Bills which are issued by Bureau of Treasury. While those that will mature between two and ten years are called Notes for example government Treasury notes or T-Notes.

Debt instruments are further classified according to its Interest Coupon. A Zero-Coupon Bond is a debt instrument that does not pay interest, but they sell it at a huge discount and the only way for you to earn is during its maturity when they redeem the bond at their par value. The difference in the price of how much you bought it at principal is your yield. That's why they call it a discount bond. Floating-Rate Bonds where the interest rate varies depending on its benchmark are usually the T-bills.

How to compute the earnings in bonds? Bond interest is usually paid on a quarterly or semi-annual basis and expressed as a percentage of its par value. If Malou bought bonds that I issued with a par value of P1,000, a fixed-rate of 6% and maturity of 5 years, she will then be paid P30 every 6 months for every unit of bond she has for 5 years.

Illustration:

Par Value / bond	P 1,000.00	
Coupon rate	x 6.00%	
Annual Yield/bond	P 60.00	or
	P 30.00	(Semi-annual]
Yield/bond for 5 years	P 300.00	

It means that for every P1,000 she invested, it will earn P300.00 for five years, that is if you wait for your investment until it matures in five years. Since a bond is tradable in the open market just like stocks, you can sell it anytime you want to. Same thing, if you miss that bond on its first issue (which is usually available 2 weeks from the time it's announced to the public], you can still buy that bond on the open market, but not at its original price but rather on its market price. Using the above example, let say that bond becomes P1,050 in the open market, how will you be able to make money by this time.

Illustration:

Par Value / bond	P	1,000.00
Coupon rate		x 6.00 %
Annual Yield/bond	P	60.00
Market Price	P	1,050.00
Current Yield/bond		0.057 or 5.71 %

You will notice that your yield has become lower than its original issue (from 6% to 5.71%], this is because currently the bond is selling at a premium, or on its quoted price of P105. Quoted bond pricing is just a jargon, just add zero to each quoted price to know its par value. If a bond is quoted at 99, then its market price is P990 for every P1,000 of face value or par value. And if bond is selling in the market above its face value, it is called at a premium. When selling below its face value it is called at a discount. When it is trading the same with its face value, then it is on par. To summarize this, look at the table below:

Face value	Price	Value	Bond Trades at
P 1,000	100	P 1,000	Par
P 1,000	105	P 1,050	A premium to par
P 1,000	99	P 990	A discount to par

Taking a closer look on bond investments, secondary market prices of bonds is influenced by the prevailing interest rate. When interest rates go up, bond price go down and vice versa. Why, you may ask? Because rising interest rates are not good for existing bond holders because new bonds will be able to pay investors higher interest rates. With that, your existing bonds will become less prominent.

With this, bond investors attempt to compute the yield to maturity on a compounded rate if they hold it up to maturity date. On this computation we assume that the coupon you will receive can be re-invested at the same yield-to-maturity rate.

$$\text{YTM} = \frac{\text{Annual coupon} + \text{or-Annualized gain or loss}}{\text{Estimated average value of investment}}$$

Again using the same example above, if that bond was now selling at the market for 90, what will be the yield-on-maturity?

Illustration:

Par Value / bond		P 1,000.00
Market Price		- 900.00
Discount		P 100.00
Years to mature		/ 5
Annualized gain	=	P 20.00
Par Value / bond		P 1,000.00
Market Price		+ 900.00
		P 1,900.00
Years to matur		/ 2
Estimated Ave.		
Value of Investment	=	P 950.00

Estimated Value of Investment is the average of the current price and maturity value.

$$\text{YTM} = \frac{\text{Annual coupon} + \text{or-Annualized gain or loss}}{\text{Estimated average value of investment}}$$

$$YTM = \frac{P\ 60.00 + P\ 20.00}{P\ 950.00}$$

$$= 8.42\%$$

In our computation, since our bond is selling at a discount, we added the annualized gain to annual coupon, but if it is selling at a premium, we have to subtract it. All is being equal if the bond were selling at a premium, the yield would then be lower and vice versa.

Bonds issued by a corporation are theoretically less secured, because we don't know what will happen to the company in the future. However bonds issued by the government to a great extent are more secure. Yes, even if you are in opposition to the current government, it has nothing to do with your bonds, for they just need to print money in order to pay you and whoever would be the new leader, he has to honor bonds issued by the previous administration. But bonds issued by corporation rely heavily on their future performance. Corporate bonds may either be secured (with collateral] or unsecured or debentures (backed solely by the reputation of the company]. Secured bonds are further classified as: mortgage bonds, equipment trusts certificates and collateral trust bonds.

Why would I choose bonds over stocks? Because ideally bonds are safer than stocks for the reason that bonds must carry some special assurance in the event of loss, unlike with stocks, your investments dive-down when the company crashes down.

Most bonds investors choose secured bonds which usually have a lower coupon over debenture bonds, which has no collateral, though even though they offer higher coupons. But if we will do a thorough analysis, the real safety of bonds or any investment in general is not based on the liquidity of assets of a corporation but on the ability of the debtor to carry out or pay its obligation. Why are we going to give up on an investment which offers a much higher interest? Just make sure you do your homework. Know the company you are investing in and then compare it side by side with the best in the industry, after which, choose the best one that offers a higher return.

Over a long period of time, investors' experience show that buying high priced high grade assets, will give you more gain than looking for larger profits from a venture of lower grade. Remember do not put your hard earned money in a substandard investments. Do not assume that an excellent performance in the past will be repeated, but it will only tell you what a rough estimate the future may bring. You must be pleased that the bond of the company that you are buying shows a very promising performance and has a good chance that it will continue to do so in the future and that they make sure that failure is a highly unlikely event for them.

VUL

I've had a very good client a few years back. I started my business with her by giving her a financial need analysis. When I asked her if she had any insurance policy, she confidently said that she had and in fact, not satisfied with her own answer, she took her policy contract and showed it to me.

To my surprise the insurance policy that she had was not the one I was expecting to see. Although, it was clearly stated in her policy how much she would get in case she broke her hips by accident, and it also showed how much her beneficiaries would get if she died by accident or natural causes; the policy that she owned which I reviewed, was in fact a form of investment. It was not just a plain life insurance policy but a VUL policy.

VUL or Variable Universal Life Insurance is a type of insurance policy that is not earning a specific rate of cash-value unlike with some regular life insurance policies which earns guaranteed cash value. With VUL, a client can invest a portion of his premium with a variety of different investment funds. Meaning, you control and can choose where to invest the cash-value portion of your premium.

Where does the name VUL come from? The Variable component refers to the client's ability to invest in separate accounts whose values vary—they vary because they are invested in stock and/or bond markets. While the Universal component refers to the fact that the premium is not a fixed amount as would be true with traditional whole life insurance policies but rather it varies within a range. In fact with some VUL products, you can add up or top-up your investment anytime you have extra money to invest. The Life component only means that it is also a form of life insurance.

Yes VULs have insurance coverage; some would be equal to 125% or even 500% of your annual premium. Think on this: if what you really need is life insurance for income protection as what we have discussed, then VUL may not be the right product for you.

Suppose you got a VUL policy and you were paying P25,000 for your annual premium. Now your policy promised you, lets just say 500% of it as your life insurance coverage. How much would that be?—P125,000! Do you think that would be enough for your family in the event something happens to you? I don't think so.

But if you use the same P25,000 in buying a plain life insurance policy then maybe, depending on your age and type of the insurance product you are looking; it can give you half or even one million pesos insurance protection.

Then I dug deeper into her policy contract, I noticed that her annual premium was heavily invested in bonds, in fact it was 80% bond and 20% in balance fund. Though in my initial analysis with her, it showed that she can be categorized as a person that can invest aggressively.

Sometimes the problem with some insurance agents is that they sell investment products and make investment allocations on behalf of their client only on plain presumption. Even worst, they translate their own investment behavior and assume that their client's investment preference would be the same as theirs. So never invest in any paper asset without first doing your investment risk assessment.

There was another case where the client was persuaded by his agent to invest in VUL. The client's first concern was about the risk of his capital. With that question, the agent readily assumed that his client was a conservative investor. So the agent put all the money into bond funds without explaining it to his client. After attending my seminar, this particular client proved to be a very aggressive investor, contrary to what his agent thought of him. What the client really meant by his question to his agent was, "What are the risks associated if I invest on that product?" He just wanted information. He was not necessarily discounting any risk especially if he knew what the rewards would be. So every time you start an investment, make sure that you raise everything you want to know with your agent, such as; associated risks, fund fees, early termination fees and other related information that they may not have told you. After all, in every decision we make, there is no one to blame but us. I don't want to sound hard. Yes, you have been deceived, you may say so, but it's still your responsibility to know where your money will go.

So is VUL a bad investment? No, in fact it is one of my favorite products to recommend. It is very similar to mutual funds. In fact the easiest way to understand VUL is by remembering:

Mutual Fund + Insurance = VUL

Like in mutual funds, you will have to choose from three different investment funds with VUL; Stock Fund, Bond Fund or Balance Fund. Though in pure mutual funds, your money after the entry fee will go entirely to investments, but in VULs you're paying not only for the entry fee but for your insurance premium as well. In fact if you compare them side by side VUL is far better.

After my client got his insurance policy, I asked if he still had some extra money to invest, it was then that I recommended that he get a VUL policy.

Supposing you had some extra money to save or to invest and you placed it in the bank or in mutual funds then an untoward incident happens to you, how much will you get? In the bank you will get your capital plus your meager earning of maybe 1%. Remember you still have to pay 20% withholding tax on it. While in mutual funds, this is what you will have: the current price per share multipied by your number of shares. That is if the price per share increased then well and good, but if not; your withdrawal value may be less than what you have invested.

In VUL, since it is a form of insurance, your beneficiary would get the insurance benefits as promised even if the value of your investments declined. So VUL is a very useful investment that augments your insurance coverage at the same time.

Although the drawback of VUL investment is; it has a longer holding period compared with other investment available in the market. So again diversification plays a big part in handling your money. VUL is not designed for your money allocated as back up fund, for it doesn't give immediate liquidity.

FINAL ANALYSIS

Now that we've discussed what bonds and stocks are, you might be thinking which of them would give you a much profitable return. If you plan to build your portfolio, you will find that you have a large amount of investment options. The two biggest portion of your portfolio would be stocks and bonds.

How to use and manage your portfolio will be your biggest challenge. In order to help you with this, you must first answer two important questions. 1] Do you want your portfolio to give you a steady stream of income or 2] are you looking for long term growth on your investment?

Bonds would give you a steady stream of income and your capital will never change over the holding period of your bond. But if you are looking for long term growth, careful selection and buying of stocks from good corporations would answer that goal.

Whatever your goal is, there should always be room for both bonds and stocks on your portfolio. For growth driven investors, having bonds will balance the risk level of your portfolio. And for the conservative investor, stocks will give you a valuable inflation protection, because history proves that stock values often rise faster than the inflation rate.

The higher gain on stocks often hedge against inflation. While your bonds serves as ballast for you to stay afloat during stock market crashes. Combining stocks and bonds on your portfolio can help you minimize risks and maximize profits.

In any paper asset investment, don't be tempted with what the company is bragging about. Anybody can claim how good their performance is during good financial conditions, we can only know who is telling the truth once the winds of economic depression blow hard. For this very reason we have to look for a company that will demonstrate promising results not only in good times but most importantly in bad times.

PART II

TAKE THE STEPS TO ACHIEVE FINANCIAL INDEPENDENCE

CHAPTER 4

THE SEVEN STEPS TO FINANCIAL FREEDOM

Every human being was created to accomplish something specific that no one else can accomplish. You were designed to be known for something special, to do something that will make you unforgettable, something that the world will not be able to ignore
Myles Munroe

I remember vividly the first day I worked as a seaman. I was a cadet then and unlike other OFWs who usually cry when they say goodbye to their loved ones at the airport upon their departure, I was actually very happy. It was the most unforgettable moment in my life at that time, for it gave me a lot of firsts—my first time to board an airplane, so it means it was also my first time to be in an airport, my first time to be in a foreign land, my first time to board a ship and above all—it was my first time to earn dollars.

In maritime school we were taught to become an officer. It was for this reason that when I first joined the ship as a Cadet or as an Apprentice, I brought a lot of books with me. In fact, the suitcase that I bought in Baclaran had gave out even before I reached the ship due to the excessive weight of the books I packed.

My very first day on board ship was a shocker, for my job was the same as an ordinary seaman, very contrary to what I expected. I told myself "this is a mistake, I'm supposed to be wearing black pants and white polo shirts with shoulder boards and doing navigational work just like what an officer should be doing". But I ended up wearing dirty and greasy overalls, chipping rust and helping the other crew members clean the ship just like an ordinary janitor back in the Philippines.

At first I couldn't understand that system, because nobody in school told me about that. It took me a month to ponder on the situation until I realized that everything had its own process and achieving success is like climbing a ladder.

If you want to reach the highest mountain you have to climb each terrain along the way and endure the challenges it offers, for you to reach your goal. The actual success of your story is not just being at the peak but how you were able to prevail on each challenge before reaching the top.

As I look back on my seagoing career, I realized that it was just right for me to experience the hard jobs that ordinary seamen experience. For it made me a good officer, it made me an emphatic leader for I know what hardships an ordinary seaman goes through and above all, it gave me a clear understanding of the practical side of my theoretical knowledge.

Just like aiming for financial freedom, you cannot have it unless you climb every step. It is for this very reason that most people who did erratic financial planning are now asking themselves "Why in the world I am so poor after working so hard all my life?"

Most of us, including yours truly, started doing the financial freedom fight haphazardly. This is the biggest mistake people can make. We usually begin a new program of changing any aspect of our lives and moving forward too fast without sufficient thought.

That behavior is also true in the way we handle our money. It is similar to starting a voyage and speeding away without a map and compass to guide you to your destination. Without those, you will usually end up nowhere, wasting your time and effort or worse, you'll find yourself in a wreckage. Sometimes we do learn but learn when?—After! So don't be obsessed with something that you lose your sense of reason that will cost you your valuable time and hard earned money.

Remember that before you embark on any venture, it is very important to know your purpose. Men and women who have been successful in any field of endeavor almost invariably have a clear vision of who they are, of where they're going and of what they really want to achieve in life. You must focus on accomplishing your great purpose. You must be decisive in all aspects of your financial goal as well as your personal purpose. Knowing what you really want, you must then do great things to get them. This is why financial planning is really important and how you should work on your plan to accomplish your goals.

Before, I thought that being emotional was an impediment to one's success for I found a lot of people who just cry when they have problems. They are weak people. But I read Anthony Robbins book: Awakening the Giant Within You, that said that we can use our emotions in our favor. Remember that emotion means energy in motion. There is huge energy behind our emotions that if we just learn how to harness it and use it in a proper way, we will accelerate faster to our goal.

The fact is that emotions are contagious. The more passionate you become in wanting to be financially free, more ideas will flow, and more people will cooperate with you in achieving your goal.

Just like any other endeavor we embark on, we must understand that there are processes or steps to be followed for you to reach financial freedom. These are the seven steps I am following and trying to teach to others regarding the subject of financial independence. These steps are:

- Get a mentor
- Generate positive cash inflow
- Manage your debt
- Build back-up fund
- Get proper protection
- Accumulate asset
- Preserve your estate

Remember that the greater power is always in favor of the person who has done the greater preparation, planning and openness to learning. Everything counts; don't leave anything to mere chance. Doing the right thing in advance and taking it one step at a time will surely bring you to your most precious goals.

STEP 1: GET A MENTOR

No one does it alone. Everything that is great and wonderful happened not because of self-sufficiency or being alone, but as a cumulative effect of the combined knowledge of all great persons that walked in this world. Finding a path to success in all areas of life require an outside force that comes from our fellow human beings who share the same mind as we do.

I highly admire how Manny Paquiao reached the top of his boxing career. A thorough analysis of how he did it will find that his achievements happened due to a combined effort of all the people that surrounded him. This is also true with other successful people in other fields of sports as well as in business or selling and marketing. We all need the knowledge and expertise of others.

I must admit that my life's success story happened late compared to some people who share the same life's trials as I do. There are known personalities who become self-made millionaires as early as the age of 30 and others even before the age of 25. They became super rich without being an employee and yet they were able to achieve financial independence at a very early age. Why?— Because they were fortunate to find their mentors.

Do you know of a successful athlete who had no coach or wasn't a member of any team in the field of sports? As a matter of fact, one of the reasons for their being constant winners is having the best coach.

There are many ways to find a coach. I started acquiring a coach by reading inspirational and motivational books as well as listening to audiotapes. The reason why I think differently compared to my friends is I read a lot. Though at the start I hated the idea of reading, whenever I see someone holding a thick pocket book I wonder how they were able to enjoy doing such a thing. Until one day, somebody introduced me to the wonderful habit of reading and how really enjoyable it is. I then realized that my previous thinking was wrong.

You may say that it's difficult. Of course it's difficult; because if it was easy, then everybody should be rich and successful by now. Remember that only those people who are willing to bear hardship and difficulties have the right to taste the sweetness of success.

If you analyze your present situation now, you might say "This is not what I want".

Try to look back ten years ago, analyze what brought you to your present situation? Ten years ago how many books have you read, how many seminars have you attended, how many persons did you ask for help to attain your dreams? If your answer is ZERO, then don't you think it's about time to drop these attitudes and change for a better one?

Whenever someone asks me how I become successful, the first thing I always recommend is to read a book that will teach about the area you want to improve in your life. Sadly, many always say "I'm too lazy to do that" or "I don't have enough time".

Ok then, given the fact that you may be too lazy or too busy, how about reading one book each month. Just one book is all I'm asking you to do. If you do read a book every month, you will be able to read 12 books in a year and in ten years you would have read 120 books. Wow, that's enormous and I promise you, if you do that, your next ten years will be different from your last ten years.

Think about this: What is the difference between these two persons; one is illiterate and doesn't know how to read while the other is literate, has gotten a high degree of education but does not spend time reading?—Nothing!

When I was still living in a squatter's area in Novaliches, they always teased me for I always carried books with me, to which I asked them in return "If you know how to read, where are you gonna' use that skill?" They would then reply "In reading street signs whenever we are going to places that we don't know, so at least we will not get lost."

I feel pity for those people who are living with that kind of philosophy. They do not see the value of reading books that will serve them just like a street sign not in the highways but on the road to life's success.

Having a mentor does not mean having a physical mentor beside you. If your excuse is you don't have connections to successful people, may I suggest that you start buying books published by highly successful and effective people on the area of life that you want to get better. That's how I started and until now I haven't stopped reading. After discovering the joy and benefits that reading gives, I don't just look for a free time to read but instead, I always give time for it. If you do the same then true enough sooner or later you will be able to meet people who can help you along the way.

Take Donald Trump, the real estate tycoon in the U.S. He is better known in his T.V. show "The Apprentice". He makes it a point to wake up 5 o'clock in the morning just to read a book until around 7 o'clock. He has all the excuse in the world not to do that for he is already very rich. But then why read more? Because if he doesn't read the new book that is out in the market and his competitor happened to read it, what do you think will happen to his business? Remember: the book that you did not read will not help you.

Just like Napoleon Hill, in his book, Think and Grow Rich, he shares his technique of having a personal mentor by using his imagination. He has an imaginary board of personal advisors which includes people like Napoleon, Lincoln, Jesus Christ, and Alexander the Great. Whenever he needs an advice for a certain decision to make, he meditates and uses his power of imagination that the members of his council of advisors were sitting at a large table in front of him. He would then ask each one of them, what is the best thing he should do to deal effectively with a particular situation. They will then begin to give him answers and insights that usually helped him to see more clearly and act more effectively.

Another way in finding the right mentor is by attending various seminars that teach financial literacy. Don't be like others who live a mediocre life, they think attending seminars are a waste of money and time. If you can afford an expensive bottle of juice or coffee, then there is no reason for you not to afford a seminar that maybe will lead you to financial independence. Anthony Robbins a well known personal motivator and most sought speaker around the world was once also a participant of one of the seminars of Jim Rohn, a well known businessman and motivational speaker and self-made millionaire.

Anthony Robbins was so captivated by the teaching of Jim Rohn that he decided to approach Rohn and ask for a job and be his student. Jim Rohn said that Anthony Robbins was so dedicated and very eager to learn. Soon enough Robbins himself became a successful motivational speaker who uses the trick of walking on fire during his seminars and the rest is history.

But don't be confused for there are lots of teachings regarding financial planning available nowadays. If you compare them side by side you'll find that most of them don't agree with each other. You pick up one book in investment or financial planning that says if you follow the steps that they are teaching it will surely lead you to richness. Then you pick up a second book that says, if you do the things that the first book says you'll end up broke. You might ask which book you should follow. No!-It is not necessary that you follow them but read them both and then make up your mind which step you will follow.

This is true with all aspects of life. Many say that a sure way to beat the stock market is by timing the market yet another investment guru says you can't time the market even if you try; in the long run you end up the loser. Jim Rohn said it best, be a student not necessarily a follower. You should take advice but not order. Don't short change yourself by not investing in your personal and financial development.

Just remember to be guided by your goal and dream. I must be honest with you that what you are embarking now is not an easy task but on a positive note it is a very exciting one. There is a saying that goes this way:

"Two men looked out through prison bars. One saw the mud; the other saw the stars."

If we keep our focus on the obstacle, we will never have the success we want. In whatever situation we are in right now, seeing the positive side of it will guide us out of our misery—look to the stars, don't look down in the mud. You can greatly improve the rate of your development by acquiring the knowledge of those people who's been there, not behind the prison bars but on the peak of success. They know the track on how to climb the crest of success. The only thing that they can provide is a map that would serve as guidance and encouragement, but the work will all depend on you. At the start it is not that rewarding but by focusing your attention on the future you'll soon realize that it was not a waste of effort. Try to see the glass as half-full rather than half-empty.

I once worked with a Swedish captain when I was a 3rd officer. I was so fortunate to have met this man—Capt. Raine Kagi. A lot of crews were afraid to work with him, for he was a typical captain, a strict and loud man. But as time passed as I worked with him on board ship, I had a chance to know him deeper, and he was different among other captains I sailed with. I was able to see his compassionate heart, and soon he was able to see my best, for he was the type of person who didn't feel insecure when he perceives that there is potential from his crew no matter how small it is.

And true enough he helped me climb the ladder of success, he promoted me to 2nd Officer in just a few months then encouraged me to take an exam for the next higher position as a Chief Officer. Yes another license, we are the only profession that requires a license from the PRC (Philippine Regulation Commission] if you want to be promoted to the next higher position. Then after passing that licensure exam, he immediately promoted me to Chief Officer, it means being next in command to the Captain. And the amazing part of it all, I was not the first person whom he helped and encouraged to aim for more.

I remember one time we were chatting on the bridge (the navigational room of the ship], he told me how he hated Filipinos, but the strange thing was that the longer he spent time with Filipinos the more he loved to work with us. I really laughed hard at that.

But what I am grateful to him for was not the chance for promotions that he gave, but the teaching he imparted to me along the way so I can reach the peak of my sea going career. He admitted that the reason he wanted to help me was because he saw the confidence in me, the eagerness to learn, the desire for success and to help others at the same time.

An astonishing aspect of human nature is that when you act in a completely self-reliant manner, others around you will often be enthusiastic to help you in achieving your goals. But if you are afraid and show lack of confidence, people will avoid you or do everything possible not to get involved with you, for they are afraid to be part of your failure.

So be confident on what you really want, believe that one day you will have it. Always trust your instinct and remember: no one does it alone.

STEP 2: GENERATE POSITIVE CASH INFLOW

After finding your right mentor to guide you, our second step to financial freedom is making sure you have a good cash flow. In accounting, cash flow represents how we use our cash either by inflow—money coming in to you or outflow—money coming out from you. The movement of our money depends on our financial activities, like spending for our basic necessities, the education of our children, paying our utilities and paying off debts—these are outflows. While activities like working for a paycheck or commission, income from investment and passive income are all considered inflows.

Obviously when we say generating a positive cash flow means that we must have more inflows than outflows. The money which we put in our pocket must be greater than the money we are taking out of our pocket. If we reach that point, then we have our financial independence. But the most bothersome question is how can we reach that point with our present income?

Definitely, depending solely on your pay check will not make you rich. Just think about this, can you reach your goals with your present income? If not, do you need to increase you inflow? Of course the answer should be yes. But how?—that's what we are going to discuss now.

There are many ways to increase our inflow, but sad to say only a very few people know and realize that this is possible to do. For what others have are all the excuses available not to do it. The first way, of course, is through the job you have right now and as you read this, I really hope you have one.

How can you increase your income in your job in the world of new market conditions? Look around, nowadays job security does not exist anymore, it's become a thing of the past, contractualization now plays a major role in the employment world. Companies either merge or is acquired by another company, and when that happens, you will never know if by tomorrow you would still have your position in your company. You don't even know if your boss today will still be your boss tomorrow. So what do you hear most of the time—job hiring or job lay-off?

So now, do you think there's still a chance to have a positive inflow with your job? Some say—Yes! If you are one of those believers then let me help you to become more positive. How can you increase your income in your present job? The answer is by increasing your value. Remember you are being paid not only by the hour but by the value you are delivering to the marketplace. Just imagine if people are being paid based on his hour then it means we should all have the same salary for we all have the same number of hours every day. But why do some people receive P300 per hour while others receive P500?

Do you think it is possible to earn P100,000 per hour? The answer is YES! How about P500,000 per hour? Yes and why not, if your value per hour will deliver results that would be worth P100 million! There are many people right now who earn that kind of salary.

But, how do you increase your value? You increase it by increasing the time you devote for self-development. Start reading a book that would help you increase the level of your competency in your job. It would do a lot of things. I'm sure you have a time on weekend. How about spending it on seminars to develop yourself?

As I told you earlier, working hard is not enough. Work hard on your self development and not on your job. Working hard on your job will give you a paycheck, but working hard on yourself can give you success. Remember that continuous learning is the minimum requirement for success in any field or profession.

Another way to increase your inflow is by using your money to make money, by investing it in active investment—meaning having your own business or investing it in passive investment—stock market, mutual fund, or life insurance company. These are what we have discussed in the previous chapter.

Make sure that every time you receive your paycheck, allocate a portion of it to be invested in two investments: active investment and passive investment.

Using other people's money is also a great idea to increase your inflow. When you use your own money to invest it in building a business, you will receive income on the effort of running that business. But if other people put their money in your business they will receive income by the risk they are willing to take in entrusting their money in your control.

Remember not all people have the idea and knowledge to put up a business, let alone run it and make it profitable. But maybe what they have is an appetite for risk by putting their money into other people's control. For that reason they just invest their money with people who have the talent to make their money grow. Just like what they said, "If you can't beat them join them", so if you can't beat Henry Sy, then invest in SM.

Another great idea to increase your inflow is by using other people's time. How does it work? The first time I heard the idea of network marketing, I was so negative about it, because I mistakenly thought it was the same as pyramiding. One time somebody approached me and introduced to me a health product that promised a lot. True enough, it worked for me and my family's health. So I got curious about the business of network marketing that I took the time to study it. Only then did I realize that what I thought about networking wasn't true at all. Since I could not contain myself regarding my own experience with that health product, I started sharing my experience to my relative and friends, when I realized that I had already started a networking business. At first it was not easy, because you had to devote time in attending seminars and inviting people, but after a while when everybody had their own businesses, then passive income started to come in.

Imagine that if you joined network marketing and you did it part time, let say four hours every day, and you were able to convince another person to do part time for four hours also, it leverages your time. It means that your friend who's doing four hours of part time, that four hour becomes your four hours too, and if recruitment goes on and on, you will never know how much you will earn by their effort. Just be careful make sure that the company you are joining is a legitimate one.

All of those were so easy things to do—increasing your value, using your money, using other people's money and using other people's time. But why is it so difficult for others to do?—because if it is easy to do, it is also easy not to do. The thing that usually holds us back is procrastination. We always leave things undone. There are lots of times that we have a great idea but we fail to act on it.

The last thing that can increase your inflow is by lowering your outflow. That is the most intelligent action to do. Plug up your financial leaks by making sure that you don't spend your hard earned money in things of lower value that does not create money but instead eats your money.

STEP 3: MANAGE YOUR DEBT

Today, there are three kinds of people: the have's, the have-not's, and the have-not-paid-for-what-they-have.

You will often hear from most financial planners and gurus, "Get out of debt!"—In fact it's their mantra. But according to Robert

Kiyosaki, that was an old and not very wise advise. Getting out of debt does not guarantee your financial freedom; on the other hand if you use debt as your ally you can reach financial independence much faster.

The only thing with debt is that you must know which one is good and which one is bad. Knowing the difference between the two is very crucial. Take credit cards, they always say to avoid it, to get your scissors and cut it literally. I say—NO! credit cards and debt are like guns; if the person who is holding it has an authority to carry it and has a sense of responsibility, then it commands respect and supremacy. But if it's in the hands of goons then you are in trouble. Debt when properly used can be your leverage to increase your money.

Debt can be categorized into good debt and bad debt. Good debt is when you take a loan and use it for some venture that will give you a much higher return than what you are paying for the interest of your loan, like small entrepreneur loans that many banks are offering right now. If you use the money you got from that loan for a small business and it gives you an annual income of let say 40% and you are just paying the bank for 12% interest, wow that's a huge spread of 28%! You were able to establish a business with low capital that gives you big income. That's what you called leveraging; using other people money to create money.

Another example is when you get a housing loan and you are paying a monthly amortization of lets say P5,000, you make it a rental property that gives you a monthly rent of P6,000. It gives you a passive income of P1,000 monthly and above all, it increase your equity on that property and the time will come when it will then be your own property and others are paying it for you. Now isn't that amazing?

It's the same thing with credit cards, you can use your credit card to buy something that you can sell in less than a month for a profit, and then pay your card from the profit of your sales on or before its due date. The card company will not charge you interest but then you were able to use your card to make profits instead. That's what I do with my business in network marketing. Sometimes I meet people who want to sell our products but don't have sufficient capital but are willing to do the business. I help them by using my credit card. That way I am able to help them and at the same time they help me earn additional passive income.

On the other hand, debts that don't give you income but charges interest are called bad debt. For example, if you take out a car loan, not just an ordinary car but a luxury car for personal use, it would cost you a lot in the long run. Not to mention the expenses the car will cost you while owning it. Same thing is true with a house and lot that you are living in, if it is on mortgage it is considered a bad debt because it doesn't give you any income but expenses instead. With credit cards, if you use it for shopping and buying things that you want, then it definitely won't give you any income-it's all expenses.

So, the third step to financial freedom is learning how to manage your debt. Whenever you are borrowing or making loan, make sure that it is a good debt,. Make a thorough calculation and study that it would give you a positive income. And at the same time minimize your bad debt. If you can eradicate it, the better.

The question now is how much debt can we tolerate? To determine how much debt we can probably get, the first thing we should consider is how much money we are making every month before taxes. It means our gross monthly income.

In a healthy financial condition, the ideal monthly debt is 36 percent of our gross monthly income. And when you are planning to get a property loan the recommended mortgage payment is 28 percent of your gross income. That 28 percent is not to be added to the 36 percent-it is to be subtracted. That 36 percent debt includes your expenses in car payments, credit card bills, personal loans, and child support or education and other bills, and yes even property mortgage.

Example:

Your Monthly Salary:	P 35,000
	x 36%
Ideal budget for Monthly Payments	P 12,600

Summary of Monthly Payments:	
Utilities Bill	P 3,500
Home Mortgage	5,000
Children Educ.	3,000
TOTAL	P 11,500

The above example shows, you have a healthy financial condition. The reason why your ideal monthly payment is only 36% is for you to have enough take home money that you can use for your daily needs. Also, having a lower monthly minimum obligation for paying debt will allow you to have enough money to save for your future.

Some financial planners recommend that before you start investing you should pay all your debts first. I would never give that same advice to my clients and friends, especially my OFW clients.

I have a sea mate, a 2nd Engr, who is paying his car loan while he is on board. He keeps all his excess money with him and plans to pay all his loan. He doesn't want to start investing, because his first priority is paying off his loan.

For a seaman, and I think it's also true for most of OFWs, their most important asset is not their brains or their skills but their health. For this reason, before we were asked to sign a contract of employment, it's very important for us to pass the medical examination first. Our talent becomes secondary to our health. The reason for this is that we become a liability to the company if we are not healthy and physically fit before we go to our work places.

What if this friend of mine prioritized paying off his debt rather than investing? What then will happen if after his vacation and it's time for him to go back onboard ship, he is not able to pass the medical requirements of the company. It will mean no more work for him. Unfortunately, he still has an outstanding loan for his car, even after sacrificing all his savings. If he will not be able to pay his monthly amortization, definitely the bank will repossess his car. Would the bank give him back the money he previously paid for the car?—NO!

It is also true with home mortgages or even with any other kind of debt. Before you pay them, first pay yourself by investing for your future. Even if they repossess or foreclose your property in a worst case scenario, you will still have money to spend while picking yourself up and try to find a new job.

But of course any excess amount of money you will earn should not be spent for unnecessary wants, but rather use it to make advance payments for your debts or loans.

The same is true with corporations and how they maintain their existence in the business world. In the corporate world they call it the *debt to equity ratio.* Investors uses it as one of the indicators on how well and stable the company is.

The Plastic Money

Credit cards are becoming a common thing nowadays. Just imagine how brilliant this invention is: a well designed small plastic card with your name engraved on it. Just swipe and you can shop anytime, anywhere in the world. No need to carry cash or sign a check. It is very convenient to use if you want to make hotel reservation, buy a ticket, gas for your car, dine in your favorite restaurants, buy books and buy things over the internet. But what is the problem?

Actually the credit card itself posses no problem but the attitude of the person who is holding it—THAT'S the big problem.

True enough owning a credit card is of great convenience. I have no question about it; as long as you use it wisely and intelligently and pay your due each month. But remember, a lot of people have ruined their finances by having this thing. They didn't have the discipline on how to use it. For some it's hard to resist, tough for them to pass the offer of a zero interest plan on their most wanted LED television. But the moment you miss a payment you might end up paying more in interests than the original cost of that television.

The most common mistake of the credit card owner is getting into the trap of paying only the minimum amount that is due on your credit card bill. It is the minimum amount that you can pay the credit card company without being penalized.

Most people think that this is insignificant for it seems that its just a small amount. But think again, if you just take a little time to calculate the total of how much you will end up paying for them compared to the original amount of your purchase, you will be surprised how huge the final amount becomes.

Why does Credit Card Company offer this option? Because it is one way for them to maintain their monthly income. Just imagine if you fall into this trap it will keep you in debt for 10, 20 or even 30 years. Instead of making them rich why not invest for your own good and make yourself rich?

To make you realize how costly the minimum payment scheme is, let me give you an example on how they compute it. Although each card company uses different calculations they use a certain percentage of the balance as a primary factor.

For our example, let us assume you have an outstanding balance of P50,000 on your card. Do you know that your account might give you an APR (Annual Percentage Rate) of 39%? Shocking isn't it, but it's true! That's the reason why they don't give you that rate as an annual figure, but instead they only give you the monthly rate. If you divide that with 12 to get the per month charge it would give us 3.25%. But more shocking of all is that, the rates we are talking about here are compounded monthly.

We further assume that your credit card company calculates the minimum payment by 3% of the balance you have or P200 whichever is higher. What does minimum payment mean? It is the minimum amount of payment required by the card company for you not to be charged with late payment fees. As long as you are paying a minimum payment you can still continue on using your card.

So therefore, your minimum payment for the first month would be P1,500 (P50,000 x 3%). Wow! How cheap, you would think, you can get your latest cellphone and pay only P1,500! But let's dig deeper. With an APR of 39% or 3.25% per month and you don't pay your bill in full for one month it means, you will be billed with a finance charge of P1,602.74 on top of your minimum payment. So, totally for the first month you will be paying P3,102.74

Illustration:
Formula for computing financial charges:
Outstanding Balance x No. of days not paying in full x ((monthly rate x 12)/365)

P50,000 x 30 dys x ((3.25% x 12)/365)
P50,000 x 30 dys x 0.1068%
P1,602.74

To further illustrate, please refer to the table below, the Credit Card Calculator:

Table 5.1 Credit Card Calculator

No. of Month	Outstanding Amount	No. of Days	Interest Rate	Finance Charge	Min Payment	Amount Payable
1	50,000	30	0.1068%	1,602.74	1,500.00	3,102.74
2	48,500.00	30	0.1068%	1,554.66	1,255.00	3,009.66
3	47,045.00	30	0.1068%	1,508.02	1,411.35	2,919.37
4	46,633.65	30	0.1068%	1,462.78	1,369.01	2,831.79
5	44,264.64	30	0.1068%	1,418.89	1,327.94	2,746.83
6	42,936.70	30	0.1068%	1,376.33	1,288.10	2,664.43
7	41,648.60	30	0.1068%	1,335.04	1,249.46	2,584.50
8	40,399.14	30	0.1068%	1,294.99	1,211.97	2,506.96
9	39,187.17	30	0.1068%	1,256.14	1,175.62	2,431.75
10	38,011.55	30	0.1068%	1,218.45	1,140.35	2,358.80
11	36,871.21	30	0.1068%	1,181.90	1,181.90	2,288.04
12	35,765.07	30	0.1068%	1,146.44	1,146.44	2,219.39
13	34,692.12	30	0.1068%	1,112.05	1,112.05	2,152.81
14	33,651.35	30	0.1068%	1,078.69	1,078.69	2,088.23
15	32,641.81	30	0.1068%	1,046.33	1,046.33	2,025.58
16	31,662.56	30	0.1068%	1,014.94	1,014.94	1,964.81
17	30,712.68	30	0.1068%	984.49	984.49	1,905.87
18	29,791.30	30	0.1068%	954.95	954.95	1,848.69
19	28,897.56	30	0.1068%	926.31	926.31	1,793.23
20	28,030.64	30	0.1068%	898.52	898.52	1,739.44
21	27,189.72	30	0.1068%	871.56	871.56	1,687.25
22	26,374.03	30	0.1068%	845.41	845.41	1,636.63
23	25,582.80	30	0.1068%	820.05	820.05	1,587.54
24	24,815.32	30	0.1068%	795.45	795.45	1,539.91
25	24,070.86	30	0.1068%	771.59	771.59	1,439.71
26	23,348.74	30	0.1068%	748.44	748.44	1,448.90
27	22,648.27	30	0.1068%	725.99	725.99	1,045.43

No. of Month	Outstanding Amount	No. of Days	Interest Rate	Finance Charge	Min Payment	Amount Payable
28	21,968.83	30	0.1068%	704.21	704.21	1,363.27
29	21,309.76	30	0.1068%	683.08	683.08	1,322.37
30	20,670.47	30	0.1068%	662.59	662.59	1,282.70
31	20,050.35	30	0.1068%	642.71	642.71	1,244.22
32	19,448.84	30	0.1068%	623.43	623.43	1,206.89
33	18,865.38	30	0.1068%	604.73	604.73	1,170.69
34	18,299.42	30	0.1068%	586.58	586.58	1,135.57
35	17,750.43	30	0.1068%	568.99	568.99	1,191.50
36	17,217.92	30	0.1068%	570.31	570.31	1,086.85
37	16,701.38	30	0.1068%	571.05	501.04	1,072.09
38	16,200.34	30	0.1068%	571.23	486.01	1,057.24
39	15,714.33	30	0.1068%	570.88	471.43	1,042.31
40	15,242.90	30	0.1068%	570.04	457.29	1,027.33
41	14,785.61	30	0.1068%	473.95	443.67	917.52
42	14,342.05	30	0.1068%	459.73	430.26	889.99
43	13,911.78	30	0.1068%	445.94	417.35	863.29
44	13,494.43	30	0.1068%	432.56	404.83	837.39
45	13,089.60	30	0.1068%	419.58	392.69	812.27
46	12,696.91	30	0.1068%	407.00	380.91	787.90
47	12,316.00	30	0.1068%	394.79	369.48	764.27
48	11,946.42	30	0.1068%	382.94	358.40	741.34
49	11,588.13	30	0.1068%	371.46	347.64	719.10
50	11,240.48	30	0.1068%	360.31	337.21	697.53
51	10,903.27	30	0.1068%	349.40	327.10	676.60
52	10,576.17	30	0.1068%	339.02	317.29	656.30
53	10,258.89	30	0.1068%	328.85	307.77	636.61
54	9,951.12	30	0.1068%	318.89	298.53	617.51
55	9,652,59	30	0.1068%	309.41	289.58	598.99
56	9,363.01	30	0.1068%	300.13	280.89	581.02
57	9,082.12	30	0.1068%	291.13	272.46	563.59
58	8,809.65	30	0.1068%	282.39	264.29	546.68

No. of Month	Outstanding Amount	No. of Days	Interest Rate	Finance Charge	Min Payment	Amount Payable
59	8,545.36	30	0.1068%	273.92	256.36	530.28
60	8,289.00	30	0.1068%	265.70	248.67	514.37
61	8,040.33	30	0.1068%	257.73	241.21	498.94
62	7,799.12	30	0.1068%	250.00	233.97	483.97
63	7,565.15	30	0.1068%	242.50	226.95	469.45
64	7,338.20	30	0.1068%	235.22	220.15	455.37
65	7,118.05	30	0.1068%	228.17	213.54	441.41
66	6,904.51	30	0.1068%	221.32	207.14	428.46
67	6,697.37	30	0.1068%	214.68	206.92	415.60
68	6,496.45	30	0.1068%	208.24	200.00	408.24
69	6,296.45	30	0.1068%	201.83	200.00	401.83
70	6,096.45	30	0.1068%	195.42	200.00	395.42
71	5,896.45	30	0.1068%	189.01	200.00	389.01
72	5,696.45	30	0.1068%	182.60	200.00	382.60
73	5,496.45	30	0.1068%	176.19	200.00	376.19
74	5,296.45	30	0.1068%	169.78	200.00	369.78
75	5,096.45	30	0.1068%	163.37	200.00	363.37
76	4,896.45	30	0.1068%	156.95	200.00	356.95
77	4,696.45	30	0.1068%	150.54	200.00	350.54
78	4,496.45	30	0.1068%	144.13	200.00	344.13
79	4,296.45	30	0.1068%	137.72	200.00	337.72
80	4,096.45	30	0.1068%	131.31	200.00	331.31
81	3,896.45	30	0.1068%	124.90	200.00	324.90
82	3,696.45	30	0.1068%	118.49	200.00	318.49
83	3,496.45	30	0.1068%	112.08	200.00	312.08
84	3,296.45	30	0.1068%	105.67	200.00	305.67
85	3,096.45	30	0.1068%	99.26	200.00	399.26
86	2,896.45	30	0.1068%	92.85	200.00	292.85
87	2,696.45	30	0.1068%	86.43	200.00	286.43
88	2,496.45	30	0.1068%	80.02	200.00	280.02
80	2,296.45	30	0.1068%	73.61	200.00	273.61

No. of Month	Outstanding Amount	No. of Days	Interest Rate	Finance Charge	Min Payment	Amount Payable
90	2,096.45	30	0.1068%	67.20	200.00	267.20
91	1,896.45	30	0.1068%	60.79	200.00	260.79
92	1,696.45	30	0.1068%	54.38	200.00	254.38
93	1,496.45	30	0.1068%	47.97	200.00	247.37
93	1,296.45	30	0.1068%	41.56	200.00	241.56
95	1,096.45	30	0.1068%	35.15	200.00	235.15
96	896.45	30	0.1068%	28.74	200.00	228.74
97	696.45	30	0.1068%	22.32	200.00	222.32
98	496.45	30	0.1068%	15.91	200.00	215.91
99	296.45	30	0.1068%	9.50	200.00	209.50
100	96.45	30	0.1068%	3.09	200.00	203.09

If you will continue doing this small payment, it would take you 8 years and four months to pay off your original debt of P50,000. And if you are going to calculate your total interest payments, it would amount to a staggering total of P50,224.87 it doubles the amount of your original balance—that's 100.45%!

To get out of credit card debt you have to find ways to pay more than the minimum offer each month. I do not recommend this but as a last resort see if you can borrow somewhere else that offers a comparatively less interest, but do so with outmost care. It might be better if you can ask help from your concerned relatives that don't charge interest at all and don't forget to promise yourself not to put yourself in the same predicament again. But I think what is most important is that you learned your lesson.

Remember that the credit card is definitely not the answer for the things that you can't afford to buy today. It is a great tool if you use it wisely, but on the other hand it can cause financial nightmares to impulsive shoppers.

GETTING OUT OF DEBT

The question now is how to get out of bad debt? I like the advice that if you fall into a pit, stop digging and find a way to make a ladder. So if you are up to your neck in debt, the first thing you should do is to evaluate what available options that you have.

Sort out your finances by eliminating bad debt. Building your savings and investment makes you a master of your own financial destiny. Getting out of bad debt will get rid of your guilt and stigma. Just imagine how that heavy weight can be taken off from your shoulder.

When I was about seven years old, I remember how terrified my mother was because of debt. She had a mountain of debt from the local "Bumbay", an Indian national that did loan shark businesses mostly in depressed areas like where we lived. These individuals thrived because they never asked for collateral. The most that they looked for is that the borrower had a small business like a small street stall where they sold vegetables or food stuff etc. or they were referred to by someone who was already a regular customer of the "Bumbay". But the downside is that they charged a huge 20% interest payable weekly. So your P5 peso loan became P6 pesos in a week's time thus the term "5-6".

Therefore people living in depressed areas find quick relief by turning to the neighborhood Bumbay for anything they lack the budget for; whether its house repair, for buying clothes, for capital to run a small business or for tuition fees of their children.

Since my mother was raising me on her own she had nobody to help her except the "Bumbay" who made an every day visit to our place on his motorcycle. In the beginning it seemed it was helping her, only to realize later that it was eating her. Until the time that she had no more way to pay her loan, the Bumbay whom she thought to be her friend became her most dreadful nightmare.

Since she knew what time the Bumbay arrives in our place, she make sure that before he arrived she would hide herself at the back of our tall cabinet. And I will sit in front of our door with a dialogue that my mom taught me "No mother here". As far as I remember that was my first English lesson from my mother.

There are many ways to deal with debt, but there are two most effective ways. One is prioritizing your debt according to its importance—making a list of all your debts and first paying the smallest one. The second, is by first paying the one that charges the highest interest.

Prioritize according to its importance, like your rent or mortgage. I'm sure you never dreamt of being one of the homeless in the street, so if you don't want to be kicked out of your apartment, taking care of your monthly rental is a good advice. The same thing applies if you are living in a house which is on mortgage. The moment you stop paying your amortization, daily charges will apply, which I'm sure you know is not cheap, that in the long run might you'll find yourself losing your property, which includes the money you have invested in it. Make sure also that you keep yourself within the budget of your utility bills like electric and water. However try to do all you can to minimize its usage.

After taking care of your most important debts, the next thing you should do is make an inventory of all your other debts and make a plan on how you can pay it off one by one. Some people start by eliminating the smallest one first. At least they can pay it off and reduce the list of their debts.

For me the wisest move is to first pay off your debt which charges the highest interest. The reason being is that the longer you keep that debt, the bigger you pay just for the interest alone. If you total the amount you have paid off, you will realize that it is more than double or sometimes triple compared to its original debt.

The moment you eliminate your debt with the highest interest, all the money that you would have been paying for that debt can now be of great help to the next debt on your list.

Another way to get out of debt much faster is to reduce the current rate of your debt. Calling your creditor and asking for a rate reduction will help much. Though they will sometimes decline, it wouldn't hurt to try. This is most applicable with your debts in credit cards and housing loans. Most of the creditors are more than willing to help you on how you can pay them back. What if they say no? You can try your luck by informing them that if they are not willing to help you by reducing their rate your option would be to transfer your balance to another card or bank with lower rates. Surely they will listen to your concerns for they need your money. After all, that is their business.

MORTGAGE REFINANCE

Another issue on debt that I want to talk about is refinancing your mortgage. When my house was on the midterm of its mortgage, a friend of mine gave me an advice to transfer my loan to another bank that offered lower rates.

During mortgage rate dips, it can be very tempting to sign up for another mortgage contract in other bank. Although seeking for a rate reduction or shortening your loan contract can be a good reason to refinance, still there are plenty of reasons why it can be a big mistake.

You have to remember that there is no such thing as "no-cost" mortgage. Once you refinance, a certain fee must be charged to you. If they offer you with a no cost refinance, definitely a slightly higher interest would be charged on your mortgage. Calculate the total it will cost you by comparing your monthly amortization and loan terms.

Seeking for a rate reduction on your monthly amortization really makes sense but as I said, don't forget the cost of refinancing.

Usually for you to get a much lower monthly payment they will just extend your loan terms. If you are paying for the last four years on your 10-year loan, refinancing it for another 10-year will give you another extra four years to pay your loan.

Illustration:

Original Loan Amount Bank A:	P	1,000,000
Annual Interest rate:		12%
Loan Period:		10 years
Monthly Amortization:	P	14,347.095
Total Interest of the Loan:	P	721,651.381
Total Payment after the loan:	P	1,721,651.4
Total Payment for 4 years:	P	688,660.56
Outstanding Loan:	P	733859.518
Refinance at bank B:	P	733859.518
Reduce Rate:		10%
Loan Period:		10 years
Monthly Amortization:	P	9,536.676
Total Interest of the Loan:	P	422,749.760
New total payment of loan period:	P	1,144,401.12
Previously Paid for 4 years:	P	688,660.56
Grand Total Payment:	P	1,833,061.68
Compare to bank A:	P	1,721,651.40
Difference:	P	111,410.28

We haven't included yet the charges on refinancing on the above calculation which usually ranges between 3-6% depending on the bank's term. Refinancing your mortgage can be a great help to ease your monthly obligation, but make sure that it really make sense in the long run before you opt for the idea.

While you are paying for all your debt, it is also a good idea to start managing your budget. Plug up your financial leaks. If you could just save the money that you are allocating for soft drinks, coffee and fast-food, it would be a big help in eradicating your debt. Not to mention the savings that you get by minimizing your texting on your cell phone. Turning off the television more and you will see how big the reduction of your electric bill is. You can now also save time instead of wasting it sitting on your sofa watching TV. If you can do that, you may now have reason to cut your cable TV subscription. Cut down on your budget for dining out. If you are working in the office bringing your own lunch will not only give you savings but an option to eat a healthy meal compared to the food you are eating in fast food restaurants. At the same time, try to increase your cash flow by using your spare hours by joining network marketing or even direct selling businesses. Soon enough you will find yourself waking up one day debt free. How wonderful that feeling is!

Remember that not all debt is bad. Debt is so powerful that it can make you rich but it can also make you poor. In achieving financial independence, learning the proper use of debt will give you leverage.

STEP 4: BUILD A BACK-UP FUND

After eliminating your bad debt, step 4 on your move to financial freedom is to start building your back-up fund. Back-up fund is commonly termed as emergency fund by most financial planners. I just prefer to call it a back-up fund to at least give a positive effect on its purpose and not to wish for any unfortunate event to happen in your life.

It is very important to have this fund before you embark yourself in any investment. If you lose your job or decide to change course on your career path, you will need some money to tide you over until you get reorganized.

It is more important to people whose job is wobbly, or people who are working on a contractual basis. Before you find your next job, your back-up fund will take care of you while you concentrate in finding the next best company for you. Of course budgeting plays a major role here. Not just because you have this fund does it give you an excuse to deplete it as you wish.

If you don't have your back-up fund you'll end up borrowing money from loan sharks who place huge interests on your loan, or worse, giving into the temptation of using your credit card which is very hard to resist. In times of need you might live on your plastic money instead of cash but after six months of not keeping up with your card bills you'll end up spending all your income paying your debts the moment you get your new job. If this happens it will surely take you a long time to get back on your feet.

Don't be tempted to use your back-up fund to buy things for your convenience like the latest cell phone a tablet pc or a new LED screen television. If you will not be careful, you'll find yourself without your funds when the real needs occur.

Where should we put this fund? Not because it is a back-up fund does it mean just shoving it under your bed or putting it in your piggy bank. You can invest your fund, why not, but the main concern is not the interest but the liquidity of your fund, meaning it should be readily accessible the moment you need it. It is the best idea to find the highest interest paying savings account. If you can find a tax free one the better. Your savings vehicle should also be very low risk for your intention is preservation of capital. Remember, interest is not your main goal, if it earns, it's just a bonus.

Avoid putting your fund into your ATMs. You may be tempted to use it once SM announces its regular sales promo, aside from the fact that it doesn't pay the highest rates of interest either. You can build your fund through money market funds, which gives accessibility and liquidity as needed. Money market funds are available through Mutual Fund Companies or UITFs (Unit Investment Trust Funds] that we have discussed in Chapter 4, The Vehicle for Road to Riches.

What if a worst case scenario hits you, you lose your job and at the same time you have a medical emergency because one of your family member needs medical attention. Just imagine how stressful it would be; thinking of the utility bills to be paid, food you need to put on the table for your family, and the enrollment time of your children. Can there be anything worse than that situation? Maybe there is, think of the people who were caught in the middle of Typhoon Millennio and Typhoon Ondoy; they lost almost everything they owned. If you are not financially prepared for situations like this, what would be your best option?

After you've poured all your tears, take a deep breath then evaluate your current situation. This is the best time for the family to gather all their strength and cooperation. Blaming and panicking won't solve anything. Evaluate what caused your financial disaster. Is it a failure to plan or a failure to implement your budget? Neglect on your job performance? Is it really the natural disaster or the total lack of financial education that caused you to be in this mess? Now would be the time that you really have to be honest to yourself, so that you can answer these questions, address the problem and find the correct solutions for the root of the problems.

The solutions that I would recommend are those that we have just discussed; prioritize your expenses, negotiate with the lender, and use your spare time to find extra money.

If you made it through that financial disaster, planning for the next one would now be easy because you've learned the most important lesson. Remember not to be naïve and that financial emergencies will surely come just as day and night happens every day. That's how important a back-up fund is. The recommended amount for this fund that you should have must be 3-6 months of your monthly expenses. That would be more than enough for you to move on, recover and get back on the right track if you experienced a financial disaster.

Let's be honest, building that 3-6 months budget would not be easy, even saving for one month would take time, let alone 3-6 months. The key is starting small. Before you spend, make sure you've already set aside a portion of your income. The moment you see the progress of your savings even how small it is you will be more inspired to reach your six months budget.

Start by putting your money in your savings account, and then as your savings grow, you can look for another vehicle that will offer a much higher interest like the money market funds or time deposits. But the key is diversification. Don't put your fund into a single account. Put your 1-3 months budget on your savings account then the rest can be on time deposits or money market funds.

Planning ahead before the real financial crisis hits will take a lot of the burden off your shoulders. There is a much greater chance of dealing with it, if at least the stress about money will be off your list. With that, your mind can now focus with creativity and effectiveness in making decisions.

STEP 5: GET PROPER PROTECTION

One may ask: "After managing my debt and acquiring enough funds for emergencies, can I now start making investments to grow my money?" Take it easy. This is not yet the best time for you to start investing unless you are done with step 5. Our next step to financial freedom is getting a proper protection in case of your untimely death.

Most people make a huge mistake by thinking that their backup fund is enough for them to be protected. Insurance protection is different from your financial emergency fund. Back-up fund is intended only for you to keep your head above water while you are trying to get back on track after losing your job. So at least you have enough money to fund all your necessities while finding a new source of income.

Insurance is your income protection. As what we have discussed in the previous chapters, it protects your income in case of your untimely death. Meaning, even if we are not around anymore, our family will not suffer the loss of their source of living. As we have discussed; it is very important to know how much you really need. Having insufficient insurance could put your family in a difficult situation, while having too much could mean you are wasting part of your money because they miss the opportunity to earn more if you had put it in investments that offered a much attractive return.

If you plan to be single all your life then, life insurance can be optional to you. Even so, it is good practice to have one for it will at least cover the basic things your family will need. It can also be used to cover your funeral expenses and estate tax if you have accumulated a considerable amount of assets.

But if you have a family of your own, meaning you are the breadwinner, then it is a must for you to have one. It should be enough to cover the immediate expenses of your family in time of your death. Enough to make sure that if they invest the proceeds of your insurance, it can send your children to school and continuously bring food on their table and provide for their basic needs. Yes, even if you are not around anymore you can still perform your obligation to them. Unless of course you don't love your family.

I know that life insurance is not cheap. At first you don't need to fulfill your full insurance needs if you don't have enough income to pay for it. But starting with at least a small amount will do a lot rather than having none at all. Well actually, there is no right or wrong answer to how much insurance coverage you really need, but the thing to consider is your goal.

Enough coverage depends from person to person. It means not leaving your family with a mountain of debt, or maybe even leaving enough for their means, or your wife would not need to work anymore when you are gone. Whatever you have started is good enough but don't stop there, upgrade your policy once you have the opportunity.

Remember, when you lose the breadwinner, you can't keep the winners, only the bread.

STEP 6: ASSETS ACCUMULATION

Finally after taking steps 1 to 5 of the basic steps to financial freedom, which are: finding the right mentor, generating positive cash inflow, managing your debt, building back-up fund and being properly protected, we are now in the sixth step, the stage where we start accumulating assets. Meaning, this is the time wherein you're going to grow your money. This is the point where you can apply the lessons that we have talked about in Chapter 3, about the different asset classes and vehicles of investment.

Trying to come up with hundreds of thousands of pesos of capital for an investment is the major reason why people keep away from starting their investment account. In the past, investing in a vehicle that offers a much higher yield was usually available only to rich and elite people. But those days are gone.

Today, equipped with the right information and education plus the help of a good mentor, you can start investing for even as low as P5,000 both in mutual funds as well as in the stock market. So there is no more reason for you not to start investing your money.

Whenever I explain this to my ship's crews when I am on board ship, their usual reaction is, "Isn't it risky to put money in the stock market?" "Yes it is", I reply. "but investing in your financial education will drastically reduce that risk".

Ponder on this: What do you think will happen to your money five years from now if you don't invest that? Can you assure me that you can hold and keep that same money you have right now? I doubt it, for if you keep that money with you, most likely you will be tempted to spend it on things that are not important to your financial goals. Which is more risky, investing your money that might lose some value during bad times but in the long run will give you a high return, or just keep it then surely lose it later on?

I don't know about you but I've learned my lessons long enough, working so hard for so long then when I look back on those years that passed, I wonder and ask myself, "Where did my money go"? I tried to calculate my past earnings and it certainly reached into the millions. How I wish I had invested at least 10% of it back then. As one saying goes, "If you're unwilling to plunge in the water, you'll never learn how to swim."

How to be incessantly motivated on building wealth? Usually people start their wealth accumulation program with all their vigor, only to find out that one day they find themselves not able to accomplish anything. The secret in keeping your fire burning is defining your goal. A kind of goal that will keep you upbeat, that you will do whatever it takes to accomplish it. Wouldn't it be simply great to have enough money so you don't have to worry?

One thing you should remember, once you have started investing your money is not to expect immediate results. That's the common mistake most people have. They are impatient. Soon enough they abandon their plans and resort to their usual ordinary way of thinking and action.

To give you an idea, consider the following tables:

How long would it take you to save up for 1 Million Pesos?

Monthly Savings	Rate of Return			
	4%	6%	8%	10%
P 100	90	67	54	46
P 500	52	41	34	30
P 750	43	35	29	26
P 1,000	37	30	30	23
P 1,500	30	25	22	19
P 2,000	25	21	19	17
	Number of Years			

How MUCH would you be able to save in 10 years at varied rates of return?

Daily Amount	Values on different Rate of Return			
	4%	6%	8%	10%
P 100	443,221.912	494,096.231	552,497.026	619,656.061
P 500	886,443.824	988,192.461	1,104,994.052	1,239,312.122
P 750	1,329,665.737	1,182,288.692	1,657,491.079	1,858,968.184
P 1,000	1,772,88.649	1,976,384.922	2,209,988.105	2,478,624.245
P 1,500	2,216,109.561	2,470,481.153	2,762,485.131	3,098,280.306
P 2,000	3,693,515.935	4,117,468.589	4,604,141.885	5,163,800.510

Beating inflation and growing your wealth cannot happen unless you have the will and the discipline to let time work for you.

The key to success in investments is persistence. Don't give up too soon. While making your way to financial independence, it is a good idea to enjoy the process and decide for yourself that you will not bring yourself back to poverty or be broke once more.

Envision yourself that you have enough money, that you can make decisions without counting how much peso you still have in your pocket, that you can achieve an early retirement, living in comfort and not be concerned whether or not you have enough money to live on your chosen lifestyle.

Financial freedom is a continuous process, a well planned endeavor to sustain your goal and to be able to help others too. Maybe right now, a majority of your time is allotted in working to make money, but just be patient and you will eventually reach the point where you will never have to work again unless you chose to.

STEP 7: PRESERVE YOUR ESTATE

When we were young, our motivation in acquiring wealth was for our own personal accomplishment. We were driven to acquire fame, power and as much material things that we can have. We defined ourselves based on what we have and what we become.

But once you've acquired all these things: fame, power and desirable materials things, you begin to look for something else— something that would define you as a higher person. And that would be "How will I be remembered once I leave this world". It is at this stage that a person becomes more concerned with his legacy to his family and to the community where he belongs.

The seventh step is very important though the most neglected one in wealth building. If you fail to make estate planning, you will end up accumulating much only to give it away later on, and even to people who are not that important to you like the government for instance.

A very wealthy man had just died and at his wake, his friends were talking among themselves when one of them asked: "How much wealth do you think he left his family?" Another friend replied "I've heard he left everything!" Gathering and accumulating wealth in this world is not about how much we can keep for ourselves. For sure we can't bring those things to wherever we will be going later. My usual answer to the question "why accumulate and then leave it later" is; it is not the amount of money or the assets you have, your true wealth is your experience—experience that you went through in order to get the things that you want. This is the only thing you can bring with you.

So while we are still here, cherish every moment. Be the best you can be so that you can influence peoples lives around you in a positive way. Build wealth as much as you can, so you can give as much as you can to as many people as you can. Just imagine how many people you will be able to help along the way.

Estate preservation is not only about making sure that the people you have chosen will inherit your wealth, but it is also making sure that it is distributed properly without leaving them in chaos.

Imagine a rich man that while on his deathbed, is invaded by his family members and relatives. They go around his house trying to secure whatever they can get; land titles, paintings, jewelries or other valuable personal effects. We've heard a lot of stories about families being wrecked by this problem. The sad thing is that this could have been prevented.

And how do we prevent such a mess? By having a plan; in estate planning, that plan is commonly known as the last will and testament or simply: a will. Every time I bring up this topic to a lot of people, especially the younger ones, they won't bother to think in the same way as the most of us. They believe that having or making a will is like inviting your own death. This is not true, for you can prevent a big problem in your family in the future by having this simple paper work.

There are two kinds of wills:

The Holographic Will and the Notarial Will.

A Holographic Will is a will entirely written, signed and dated by the hand of the testator—you. There is no required formality in writing it; you can even leave some advice to your children or your spouse in your own words on how to live their life without you. Holographic Wills do not need any witness when you write it.

While the Notarial Will on the other hand, is written by someone else in your presence, usually your lawyer, and it is attested and subscribed by three or more credible witnesses in your presence, and signed by all involved. Each and every page except the last must be signed on the left margin by the testator and his witnesses in the presence of each other. Each and every page of the will must be numbered correlatively in letters placed on the upper part of each page. And it must be acknowledged before a notary public by the testator and all witnesses.

But whether you leave a will or not, your assets must still be distributed. If you leave a will then the law will honor it as long as you do it according to what the law prescribes. This is what is called as Testamentary Succession. However, if you fail to make a will then the estate will decide in your behalf, it is called Intestate Succession.

Testamentary Succession

In the Philippines, it is important to remember that the law regarding inheritance is biased towards the heir. For a certain part of the estate of the deceased cannot be freely disposed of, because the law reserves that for the "compulsory heirs". Heirs are classified as:

Primary—legitimate children and/or descendants

Secondary—legitimate parents and/or ascendants, illegitimate parents **Concurring**—surviving spouse, illegitimate children and/or descendants

Collateral—brothers, sisters, nephews, nieces and relatives up to the 5th degree

How does it work? Primary heirs are preferred over Secondary heirs to receive inheritance. Secondary heirs receive only in the absence of Primary heirs. So it means that if I were going to make a will, my first priority should be my children not my parents anymore. My parents can only receive an inheritance if I have no children at all.

Concurring heirs generally inherit as compulsory heirs, together with primary or secondary heirs. With or without your legitimate children, your surviving spouse will still obtain an inheritance. The same is true with your illegitimate children if you happen to have them, even if your legal wife does not want to, they will still have their own share.

Omission of one, some or even all of the compulsory heirs shall annul the institution of heir, in legal term it is called preterition. If you eliminate any of them without legal basis, or even if one of them does not receive their fair share according to what the law requires, then it will invalidate your will.

You might ask: "What about those stories that *telenovelas* usually portray, that they just disinherit their prodigal child when they are upset?" That is a misconception, because in our law system, when it comes to inheritance, it prioritizes the compulsory heirs. Does it mean we cannot disinherit our heirs? We can, but you must do it in express provision provided by the law. If you state the reason why you want to disinherit any of them and as long as the reason is valid in accordance to what the law provides, then you can disinherit them. But you cannot make a will and just remove your compulsory heirs just because you don't want them to be included in it. If you do so, then it will nullify your will.

Collateral heirs are your siblings, nephew, nieces or relative up to the 5th degree, inherit *only in the absence of compulsory, secondary and concurring heirs.* For example the deceased or the estate owner left a fortune but it so happens that he has no family of his own and his parents are both gone already, then collateral heirs will now come into the picture. But unlike compulsory heirs, with collateral, you can only give to those whom you want to give, it is not necessary that you must give to all your collateral heirs. But for you to do that you must write a will.

To prepare your will, the first thing that you should do is to take a full inventory of your assets. It includes all tangible assets like real property, car and other things of value, as well as your liquid assets like money in the bank, investment in the stock market, bonds, or mutual funds and the value of your business. You must also know how much liability you have, like mortgages and loans. Take the difference between your assets and liability and that is the total estate that you have to include when you plan to prepare your will.

Basically your total estate in will preparation is divided into two portions. Under the New Civil Code they are called Legitime and Free Portion. Legitime is a part of your total property that is reserved only for compulsory heirs that are mentioned above. It cannot be disposed to others except to the compulsory heirs only.

While the Free Portion is the remaining property left after distributing your Legitime. This time you can give it to whoever you like. If you are married and have children, you can also give to your aging parents using this free portion, so you don't need to worry about them even if you're gone. It can also be given to your compulsory heir to increase their inheritance if you want to, or to somebody who is close to you like your yaya or any relative who you think need some financial support. Or if you have a philanthropic heart you can give a portion of your wealth to your chosen charity.

The Philippine Civil Code about Legitimes

There are certain instructions on how to distribute our estate to your compulsory heirs. As I have said the law is biased to our heirs; if you omit one of them or if you favored one of your children, then the others can contest it and it will lead to your will invalidation. To simplify it, let me explain this law in this scenario:

If you have only one legitimate child he/she is entitled to the 50% of the estate. But if you have two or more legitimate children then they will share this 50% equally among them.

Your spouse is entitled to 25% of your estate if you have only one legitimate child. But if it happens that you have 2 or more legitimate children, then your spouse will receive the same portion as what your children will receive and the rest will go to the free portion of the estate.

If you have illegitimate children, their share will be taken from the free portion. The share of each illegitimate child consists of 50% of that of a legitimate child.

If you don't have legitimate children, but happen to have an illegitimate child, then your parents as your secondary compulsory heirs will receive that 50% instead of them. Then you can dispose of the remaining 50%, 25% of that will go to your illegitimate children, 12.5% will go to your spouse and the remaining 12.5% goes to the free portion.

Let's take Armando as an example. Armando is living with his four children and his wife Anita. He is making a draft of his will, so how will he distribute his assets? The 50% of his estate will be reserved equally between the four children; it means each will receive 12.5%, whilst Anita takes the same 12.5% of Armando's total estate. So now, the total asset that Armando already given was 62.5%, so it means he still has 37.5% left to be given.

This 37.5% is now what we call free portion that Armando can freely give to anybody in accordance to his will. He can give it to his aging mother whom he is supporting. If he thinks that the 12.5% of his estate is not enough for his wife and children he can still give it to them or if Armando favors one of his children above the others then this is his chance to add it to him.

Intestate Succession

If you are one of those few people that still believe that will preparation is a taboo, your failure to do it will not stop your family from inheriting what you have left. In the absence of a will, the law will designate intestate heirs. If you are a legitimate child of your parents and accumulated a sum of asset and you leave this world, the following is the order of succession that the state will do:

Legitimate children or descendants
Legitimate parents or ascendants
Illegitimate children or descendants

Surviving spouse Brothers and sisters, nephews and nieces
Other collateral relatives within the fifth degree
The State

While if you are an illegitimate child the order of succession that the state will do is as follows:

Legitimate children or descendants
Illegitimate children or descendants
Illegitimate parents (other ascendants are excluded]
Surviving spouse Brothers and sisters, nephews and nieces,
The State

Same with testamentary succession, the surviving spouse and the illegitimate children of the deceased are considered as concurring heirs and they will receive, as a general rule, together with the primary or secondary heirs.

Just remember, if you fail to make your own planning and you leave this world without a will, the state will still distribute your assets. Once the government does the distribution, the free portion is eliminated, and even a member of your family that you don't like to have a piece of your assets will now have a part of it.

But if you plan ahead, you will not leave them in turmoil. Remember, the most important wealth you have is your family and your family must also realize that their most important asset in life is having the love and support of one another that even if you leave them with nothing at all, as long as they have each other, they can still easily cope with their loss.

I believe, the lesson of love will still be your most valuable inheritance for them. You can leave this world without any material thing for them, but without love to guide and strengthen them together in your absence, even if you are able to give them the whole world—it will all be meaningless.

I read an article in the Manila Bulletin entitled "US billionaires pledge fortunes to charity" [August 2010]. Two of the world's richest men—Warren Buffet and Bill Gates was inviting all US billionaires to pledge at least half of their wealth to charity, and a lot of US billionaires joined that call. One of the billionaires is Pickens, an energy tycoon that said: "I'm not a big fan of inherited wealth. It generally does more harm than good".

Leaving your family, especially your children the lesson of how you became successful and how you acquired whatever you have now is the greatest asset they can get from you—the How and not the How much. Share to them the knowledge of how you made it, because if you teach them that, then you can give money away to others or to your chosen charity for now they will also know how to do it.

Becoming wealthy is not about how much you have made but what kind of person you have become.

THE PYRAMID OF WEALTH ACCUMULATION

The more money you have, the more problems you have. I went from having no money to making comparatively a lot and all I've had is problems. Life was simpler when I had no money, when I just barely survived.

Madonna
U.S. pop singer
and film actor.

When I was still in college studying to become a seaman, I started knowing a lot of people who were in the maritime industry; from an Ordinary Seaman up to a Captain. I always envied them for being so lucky to earn that much, especially those in the higher positions like an Officer or Captain in particular. There was once a Captain that I was always envious of. At that time I thought he had everything. He had a beautiful car, a big house and all of his children were studying in exclusive schools. Whenever he was on vacation, I always saw them going to the mall carrying a lot of shopping bags; buying things they wanted to.

After 15 years, I met that captain again, he's now retired. But he's not the same person I knew before. He looked so depressed living the opposite life that he had before. He still has the same house but unlike before, it now looked like a haunted house in a horror movie. When you look at the garage area of his house, it is empty unlike before, his third car stayed outside the fence because his garage was already occupied by his two other cars.

I was shocked to learn that all his children did not finish college. They got married early and all of them were staying with him. In short he was totally broke and considered himself a failure. When I learned what happened to him, my biggest fear became: "Am I going to be like him when I retire?"

One of the most useful tools in financial planning is to understand the pyramid of wealth accumulation. It's so simple yet very few people understand it and with that, a lot of us miss the opportunity of having a much secure financial direction.

It's like when King Sneferu of Egypt who built the modern pyramid with smooth sides during 2575-2467 BC. With his technique, the modern pyramid was developed because each level was slightly smaller than the one it is laid upon. Prior to that, his architects had designed it with an angle of 60 degrees to the ground so that when the pyramid rose, it started to sink due to its angle and the weight of the stone. The moment you make your top and its succeeding levels almost equal to the base, your pyramid will sink to the ground due to the heavy weight of the load above the base.

How about constructing a pyramid starting from the top level, do you think it will work? I know you will think that it's a stupid question. But isn't it that most of us commit the same mistake? We start building our financial pyramid from the top or from the middle.

The pyramids of Egypt were built to preserve the dead kings and queens, now with the Pyramid of Wealth Accumulation (figure 5.3]; it is designed to preserve not dead people but assets.

To understand the pyramid of wealth accumulation, let us discuss it level by level.

Level 1 is about financial security. It means protecting yourself and your family from whatever will happen; protection against the loss of the breadwinner or income continuation, health protection and protection of your properties.

Level 2 is wealth build-up. Means growing your money and making your money your slave not the other way around. You can achieve it by investing your money wisely and diversifying your investment.

Level 3 is wealth continuation. Means making sure that whatever you built will be passed on to your next generation.

THE 3 LEVELS OF THE PYRAMID OF WEALTH ACCUMULATION:

LEVEL 1-FINANCIAL SECURITY

This is the most crucial stage in building your pyramid, the strength and stability of what you are building depends heavily on this first level. When you are building a skyscraper, the longest stage is digging the foundation. Then after completing the foundation, everything will happen fast.

How deep your foundation is will depend on how high your building will be. With the financial pyramid, how wide or big your first level will be the defining factor of how strong and stable the succeeding stages will be. This will be the support of your financial goal. For that we call it basic security and contingency fund.

Financial security composes of:

Back-up fund
Basic retirement fund
Children education fund
Health care

Disability Income
Property and casualty coverage

LEVEL 2 WEALTH BUILDUP

After ensuring your financial protection, it is now time to start growing your money, to make sure that while you are working for money, one day money will work for you. But how do you build your wealth?

In building your wealth your first investment should first go to your personal education. Knowing the roadmap to success is very important. Making a wrong turn will cost you a lot of money and the most expensive of all items: time. Remember that there is no shortcut. If you understand well how money works, you can use it to your advantage.

Wealth build-up is not a haphazard process. It should start from the basics to a more complex procedure. The more complex the process, the higher the financial education you must have. And the more complex it becomes, the less wide it should be. Just like building a pyramid, the higher the level it goes, the narrower it becomes. These are the four levels of wealth build-up:

Short Term Investment

- Back-up Savings
  (Recommended: 3-6 months of your gross monthly income)

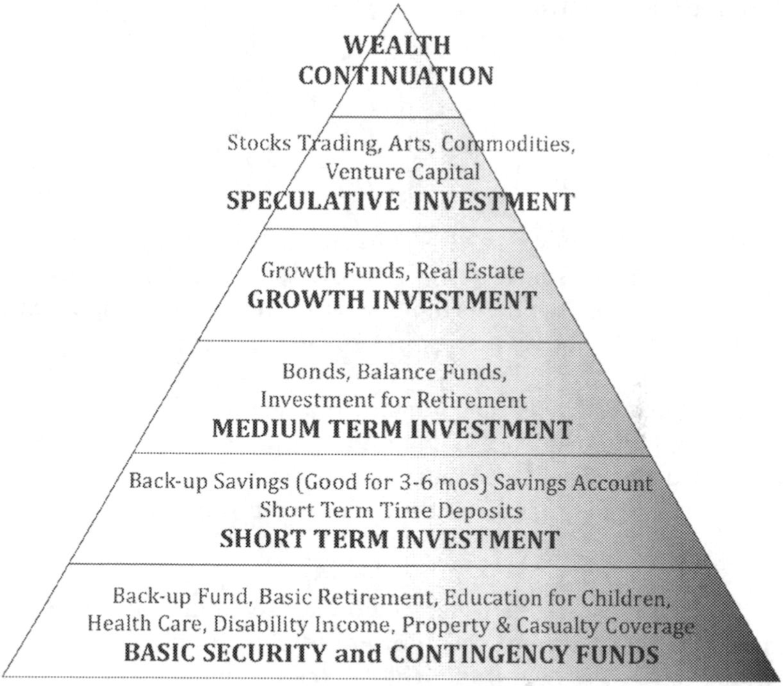

WEALTH
CONTINUATION

Stocks Trading, Arts, Commodities,
Venture Capital
SPECULATIVE INVESTMENT

Growth Funds, Real Estate
GROWTH INVESTMENT

Bonds, Balance Funds,
Investment for Retirement
MEDIUM TERM INVESTMENT

Back-up Savings (Good for 3-6 mos) Savings Account
Short Term Time Deposits
SHORT TERM INVESTMENT

Back-up Fund, Basic Retirement, Education for Children,
Health Care, Disability Income, Property & Casualty Coverage
BASIC SECURITY and CONTINGENCY FUNDS

Figure 5.3 Pyramid of Wealth Accumulation

- Savings account
- Short term time deposits

Medium Term Investment

- Bonds
- Balance Funds
- Investment for retirement

Growth Investment

- Growth Fund
- Real Estate

Speculative Investment

- Stocks Trading
- Arts
- Commodities (Oil, gold, metals, etc.]
- Venture capital

On this stage, having a very reliable mentor is very important. Seek advice from somebody you know who has done it before. Reading books related to the topic of investing and growing wealth will be a big help for you.

One book I always recommend to anybody who's interested in financial independence is the book entitled **The Richest Man in Babylon by George Clason.** It is a very interesting book as it is written in a story form that even your children will surely appreciate.

Don't be stupid like others who choose to lose an immense amount before they got the courage to seek advice from other people. But be very careful of the advice you will get, make sure that the person giving you the advice is after to your welfare not for his own advantage.

LEVEL 3 WEALTH CONTINUATION

I'm sure that all of us want to build something that we want to have in the long run, though we must accept that nothing in this world is permanent. Wealth continuation is the concept that whatever we are building today, one day we will have to pass the torch to somebody we really love and trust.

This is the manner of taking into account the unavoidable risk of the untimely death. It takes great effort and risk to build the pyramids of Egypt, but it is another thing to make it last and stand the test of time; to last forever and pass it on from generation to generation.

THE FINANCIAL DISASTER

Many people make the mistake of building their pyramid in a very unintelligent way. The moment they start to earn extra money, many are immediately attracted to invest in real estate without having any protection at all in the event of a critical illness, which if you refer to our pyramid, real estate should be in stage four. So the moment they have a critical illness, they sell their investments even for half the value of their original price just to cover their hospital and medical bills.

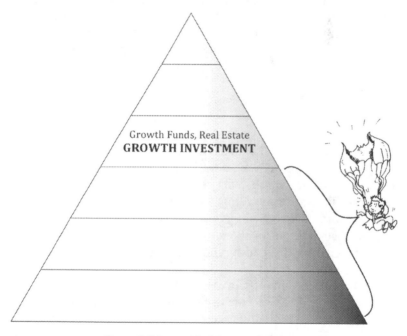

Figure 5.3 Pyramid of Financial Disaster

OFW's are the usual victims of this unfortunate scenario; they forget that their most valuable capital in working abroad is their health and physical condition. Not protecting your most expensive asset is a sure road to disaster. And worse, some people start trading in the stock market without a back-up fund. The moment the market crashes and it also happens at the same time they lose their jobs due to the effect of market depression and mass lay-offs, they sell their shares for a loss. They thought that the stock market is a big casino to gamble in, in order to secure their financial future.

Remember, starting your wealth accumulation in random order against the financial pyramid will surely lead to the collapse of your financial goals. The distance of your current financial level right now to the base (Basic Security and Contingency Fund] is the amount of impact it will cause you the moment your finances collapse (figure 5.4]. Like most seamen I knew, they were deceived to believe that the best investment they could have is real estate. They were afraid to invest for their basic protection for the fear that one day, insurance companies would be insolvent just like the other pre-need companies.

What most of them did is to buy real estate, every time they come back to the Philippines. They thought that their assets are well diversified for they invested in agricultural lands in their provinces, house and lots in Metro Manila and even condominium units in prime areas like in Makati and The Bonifacio Global City which used to be part of Fort Bonifacio. The moment they get injured or have a critical illness and forced them to retire early, they were left with no other choice but to sell their properties at a bargain price in order for them to survive and support the need of their family specially sending the children to school.

I have nothing against investing in real estate. In fact, if you truly understand how to make money in real estate it is a very profitable investment. But make sure that when you invest in real estate, you are after a positive cash flow or a passive income. Meaning, even if you are paying a monthly amortization, the money that is coming from the property you acquired is much greater than the money you are paying the bank. With that, even if you stop going abroad or stop working on your job, you have no fear for you will still be able to pay your amortization and have a passive income at the same time.

Don't invest in real property hoping that the agent's presentation to you will come true, that one day your property will appreciate in market price. Look for passive income not capital appreciation.

Never risk your children's education fund on a very speculative investment. Make sure you invest it into something that would give you an almost guaranteed return and still preserve your capital. Never mind if the yield is not that attractive. It is better to make sure that your beloved children will one day have their money for school than put it into a promising investment and pray every day that one day your money is still intact by the time you need it.

PART III

GROW YOURSELF AND LIVING LIFE TO THE FULLEST

CHAPTER 5

PERSONAL MANAGEMENT

We are what we repeatedly do.
Excellence, then, is not an act, but a habit.
Aristotle

I was watching TV one evening when I landed on a channel that was showing a cooking show program. I adored it for it was not the traditional cooking show that I usually see on T.V. It was a combination cooking show and game show called the Iron Chef America. Two chefs were competing on who would be able to make the best dish with a secret ingredient that was revealed to them just before the countdown began, and the chefs were given exactly one hour to do the cooking.

It was exciting to watch how the chefs maneuvered around the kitchen. They did their cooking just like it was second nature to them, without even pausing for a second to think on what ingredients to combine with the secret ingredient. They knew what spices to use to give the secret ingredient more emphasis. And most admirable of all was that they were able to finish their cooking, present their cuisine in a very attractive way, just in before the timer stopped. It was simply amazing to watch.

Life's struggle for success is like competing to be the Iron Chef. You must know your secret ingredients, so that when the time is given to you, you can easily maneuver your life's success. It is true in all areas of life, whether in career, relationships with people, relationship with God and yes—even in the area of finance.

It is also important to be familiar with the other ingredients in your surroundings; their uses and their properties. And above all you must know how to use different spices to make life more vibrant and enjoyable.

Take the dish "pakbet" for example. A local cuisine popularized by Ilocanos, it is an assortment of different vegetables, meat and seafood. Or if you don't know what "pakbet" is, then think of your favorite viand. But try eating its ingredients separately I doubt if you'll be able to enjoy it.

It's the same thing with life's success, it is an art of combining different ingredients at the right amount and in the right order. Just like in cooking, in life you don't need to experiment at all, for a lot of people who have done it in the past, have left us a legacy or trail to follow just like a recipe.

I heard Julie Yap Daza said it once in her cooking show, that for you to have a beautiful and delicious cake, you must measure your ingredient with full accuracy or else it will collapse. Isn't it also true with life? You must measure all areas of your life with full accuracy or else you will not be successful with your finances or with your family or whatever. You might be successful in your career but what about with your relationship with God. Or you may give all your time in your church but neglect your obligation with your family especially in providing food on your table.

After discussing the different tools for us to be successful with our finances, it's time to discuss the different areas of life's ingredients that was entrusted to us and its uses. For people to be really successful in all areas of life, he or she needs to master the use of his or her TIME AND MONEY.

We will discuss the value of time management and how to set priorities so that everything you will dowill be the most efficient use of your time in achieving your life's objectives.

We will discuss money as well; how money works, how not to feel guilty when accumulating wealth and how to think of abundance and which I think is the most important factor for life's success, how to be spiritually comfortable being rich.

Like the "Seven Steps to Financial Freedom" in Chapter 4, if you first take a baby steps, practice and then master this personal management that we are going to discuss, you can surely reach your goal. It's like having a magic lamp that once you stroke it, you are entitled to wish but the only difference is—it gives you a never ending realization of wishes. And every time you ask, the genie of the lamp will surely reply:

"Your wish is my command . . ."

TIME MANAGEMENT

"Time is a companion that goes with us on a journey.
It reminds us to cherish each moment, because it will never come again.
What we leave behind is not as important as how we have lived."

Capt. Jean-Luc Picard
Played by Patrick Stewart
from the film
"Star Trek: Generations"

The most challenging part of success in personal management is time management. Remember, time is more precious than money. You can create more money later in your life but not time. When you fail in money matters, you can easily get back on your feet. And if you are properly equipped with things and attributes needed to make money, you can get it back if ever you have lost it.

However, once time is gone, you can never recover even a single second of it. Most people get reluctant with time for they don't recognize this simple reality. As time passes, we accumulate tons of money, so we might as well take advantage of time because when the opportunity pass by it will never return in you life.

Don't just be an average person. Remember, life is not simply the passing of time. It's about the question of what experiences to put on your time while it passes.

Think, what is the difference between you and Henry Sy, Manny Villiar, Go Kung Wei, Lucio Tan or other successful and self made millionaires? If you dig deeper you'll find that it's not really much. I believe that God created man with an equal opportunity available to them—that is time.

These people I mentioned, me and you, equally have 24 hours each day. The defining aspect among us is not those 24 hours that we have but *what we do* with our 24 hours.

Time is a democratizing feature of life. The first time I learned this philosophy I said to myself "Wow that's amazing!" Because most of my previous time was spent in complaining, blaming and being jealous of others; of those successful people and I found myself oftentimes cursing them.

Be honest with yourself. List down on a piece of paper, how you spend your 24 hours in a typical day. Pick a normal working day, so that you can have a view of your typical daily life. Start from the moment you wake up until you go back to your bed to sleep at night.

Analyze what you have written. Definitely if you add up all the time that you have spent, it won't give you a result of 24 hours. So the question is how much time did you spend in sleeping? Where do you spend your time if you are not working? How much time do you spend in traveling from your home going to your place of work and back again to your home? How much time do you spend with your family? How much time you have allotted in watching TV? Above all with whom did you spend your time?

How much of your day was spent doing something that will contribute for your life goals? I think that is the most important question to ponder. Most people often ask how their life became miserable but they never ask how they wasted their most precious possession: time.

Yes, you may be a good child, a good sibling, a good member of your community and a good member of your church. But if you are not a good manager of time what is the chance of you becoming successful? Remember, success is biased to those people who know how to give value to the most major aspect of success which is time.

Success is relative for each of us. Some will say that they can consider themselves successful if they already have their dream car, dream house or maybe even a million pesos in their bank account. Others define success based on the kind of relationship they have with their family.

Or some will say that success is if you have reached the top of the corporate ladder, or recognized in your community or in your church. However, how you define success is up to you.

Never let other people define success for you. But that is what most people do to themselves. They never stop competing with others, constantly comparing or as they say in America: always trying to keep up with the Joneses.

Knowing yourself is winning half of the battle but don't deny yourself with the things mentioned above. It is a good way of living if you have allocated a portion of your time for yourself, your family, your health and your career, balancing the social, spiritual and financial aspect of your life. That is the most effective way of living.

Go back to the list of things you do every day. Do you suppose you can achieve the most effective way of living if you continue to spend your time on the things that least matter to you? The most common mistake of people is to mix things up. When they are at work they think of their family which reduces their productivity and when they are at home they think of their work and worst of all is that they bring their work home. Focus on one task at a time to be able to accomplish more.

We say that time is so precious, so therefore it is our duty to protect things that are precious to us—and that includes our time. Mastery of the use of time involves not only time management but time protection as well. On this day and age we are easily robbed of time due to the increasing and unwanted interruption and distractions; cell phones, the internet and social networking are some of the most notorious time stealers. They said that technology makes our life easier, then why is it that we are now more short of time than ever?

Some even say that for you to keep pace with the fast changing world you must learn how to take advantage of the internet. But one thing I've noticed, is that it is so easy to be online but off-track of your goal. Just count how much time you spend on clicking and uploading pictures and unimportant messages on todays' rampant social networking sites. What's worse is, it even reduces the productivity of most employees who are always online. We are living in a very competitive and uncertain world, so instead of wasting your productivity in your work place, try to think of things that will make you ahead of the others professionally.

The internet is a very useful tool for today's competitive world but you must know how to use it to your advantage—don't be a slave of it. Napoleon Hill's book says "Think"—Think and Grow Rich. But some people say we must get online for opportunities to become rich have shifted online. But Napoleon Hills book clearly says let's Think (first, THEN] and Grow Rich.

Think of the things where you can use your time properly, think of the new opportunities that life might give you, and think of a better way to be creative, not just busy. Being busy does not necessarily mean being productive and effective. Consider this, every minute you waste is equivalent to every minute you have deprived your family of your time.

There is a truism that life is not all about money but it's just a part of how to make life worthwhile. You must spend more time in the area of your life that matters to you most. It's not good to have all the money in the world but then neglect your health and suffer in the end.

Don't deprive yourself of spending the fruits of your labor. You have the right to enjoy life using the money you have earned. But don't do it in a way as if money will come forever, that is very naïve thinking.

When I was still in college at the Philippine Maritime Institute, my school was located in Sta. Cruz Manila. Going to and from school, I would always pass by people living in "home along da riles" (literally translated: homes along the train rails-it was the title of a very popular comedy sitcom in the 90s. These were almost always squatter shanties lining the rails] in Blumentritt. I sometimes envied them for they did not seem to worry about their living conditions. But on the other hand, I also kept thinking "Is this the kind of life I want to have?"

Life is not just a passing of time, life is a journey of success and failure; a collection of memories, it's joy and sadness which makes us significant human beings.

Remember the degree of success that people will have is not based on the time he has, but on what he put in his time. Do you want to be like the successful people I mentioned? Then, it's time to put something in your time that will make you also successful.

You have to make your mind up and set clear priorities in all areas of your life: either in self-development, family, health, social, spiritual and financial. Always align yourself with the activity that will give surety on the greatest results in important areas of your life—happiness, great health and long term prosperity. Every sacrifice you make today will define your life in the next five years, ten years and so on. Be an effective time manager and you will be rewarded with compounded interest in the future that lies ahead of you.

"Time is the most impatient of all. It waits for no one."

FINANCIAL MANAGEMENT

Ask yourself, "What have I done with my life? What have I contributed to the human race? What have I really left for the next generation to know that I was here? Have I worked hard and accomplished little?
Myles Munroe

Whenever I conduct a presentation about financial planning and investment, the first objection that I usually hear is:

"That is not for me, I don't even know how to fit in my family's basic needs with my current income, what more in investing and financial planning."

That's the usual excuse of people living an ordinary life and having an ordinary dream. For they are just trying to live according to the wages they are receiving and it's minimum wages dictated by the government or worse, maybe less than that.

But I was surprised when I conducted the same seminar in my ship when got back on board. I gave them a free financial education seminar during one of our free times on a Sunday afternoon. Most of them gave the same initial reaction as with people working ashore in the Philippines—they believed that their money was not enough for them to invest!

The way we handle money is the way we learned what money is. The nagging question is, "When did we learn the subject about money?" Sad to say, money management was hardly ever taught in school, if it was, it is not enough.

Look at the people who took the profession that has direct relation to the subject of money—bankers, accountants, business managers, finance officers. Most of them end up being broke on their retirement. I have known a few people who are hiding from the law because they embezzled money from their company. They sold out their selves and souls just for money.

We learn financial management from our most basic of schools—our family or to be precise, from our parents. Do you have a problem with money? Is money your major issue why you are unhappy with life? Then look at your parents. Does the same question give you the same answer?

When do we have to start managing our finances? When should we teach our children in handling money? Financial management does not require that you must have excessive money to start with. It should start the moment you receive money either from your job or allowance from your parents. Meaning that the moment you have a source of income, that income should be well taken care of, not just for the day's expenses but for future concerns too.

If you can't manage the small amount of your income what is the chance that you can manage a much bigger sum? Perhaps that may be the reason why most people are not able to accumulate a bigger sum due to their failure in managing a small one. Teach your children financial management even before you give them their first peso.

The subsequent discussions are perhaps the highlights of this book, in terms of financial management and the way to financial freedom. We are going to discuss the formula in investing our money for us to reach our various financial goals. We will tackle the issue of the holistic side of money, as well as how money works and how to use it for our advantage. We will also deal with topics on why people are failing financially.

WEALTH FORMULA

"Wealth is the ability to fully experience life."
Henry David Thoreau

There was a story about two men who have been good friends since their childhood; they are Geraldo and George. Both of them grew up in the same community but were separated by their living conditions. Geraldo was living on the west side of the community; a subdivision because he belonged to a middle class family. While George lived on the East side where the shanties or "squatters" were because he came from a poor family.

Geraldo lived a life of abundance: his mother was a government employee while his father worked in a big factory near their community as one of the operation officers.

On the other hand, George's mother was a laundrywoman and his father was a known carpenter in their community. To help his family, during his spare time after school, he joined the other kids in their neighborhood in working as "mangangalakal ng basura" or what are known as scavengers. Every morning he wakes up as early as 5 a.m. to sell pan de sal (salted bread] coming from a nearby bakery. He delivered pan de sal to every door step of their neighborhood.

Geraldo studied in a well known private school in their town from elementary until high school, while George went to a public school on their town. After high school Geraldo went to a well known university in Manila, while George also studied hard to earn the scholarship offered by their city mayor for him to be able to go to college. He also worked to earn some money for his studies.

What do you think would be the ending of the story of these two good childhood friends? Who among them became the first to be rich and wealthy?

The financial aspect of each one of us is a struggle like a wheel of fortune—that's what we heard from our grandparents and parents, that sometimes it's up and sometimes it's down. But for some, they believe that their downs are more frequent than the ups. But my opinion is much more sophisticated than that. If you believe in the "gulong ng palad" or wheel of fortune, then you don't believe that you can have a full control of your life.

Why do people who have been in the peak of their career and have attained financial success end up back to as low as their original condition or sometimes much worse than before?

You may be working on the wrong things, exercising the wrong deeds to attain your wants and temporarily succeeded by mere accident or by high merits of the condition at that given time. On the other hand you might have stumbled on the right method and be successful only to wake up on the same ditch that you hated before. Why is this so? It's because a person fails to reduce the principles and the lessons behind his success and failure to a formula.

To be honest, I am not fond of numbers. But one thing I've noticed, all the most complex human problems can be solved by using a formula. Most of the great thinkers are those who were able to come up a formula that could solve human needs and problems, from mathematical problems, food problems (that made chemists and food technicians very much in demand), physiological problems and human behavioral problems. It's also the same thing with in the financial aspect, formulas works.

There are four levels of formulas working in our society when it comes to handling and growing money.

Level 1-poor people,
Level 2-ordinary people
Level 3-rich people
Level 4-abundant people

Please don't misinterpret me; I'm not here to demean poor people, when I say poor people it doesn't mean people who are living below the poverty line. There are lots of people living in the most expensive and most exclusive subdivisions but we can not consider them rich, but poor. The amount of money that you have right now will depend on what formula you are using to live with it. It doesn't matter what educational background, profession and source of income you have—it really depends on the formula you are using.

LEVEL 1-POOR PEOPLE

FORMULA NO.1:
INCOME-EXPENSE = SAVINGS

Being rich is not determined by the income you are receiving but on what you keep from your income. Everybody wants to be rich, but the question is how to do it with our present financial condition. The above formula has been mastered by the poor people. I will say it again this is not to degrade those people who are trying to survive their three meals a day and living in a very depressed area. I don't want to appear without compassion on their situation. For, I myself came from that very situation before.

When I say poor, these are the people who are not poor on the outside but poor in the inside. Remember, our outside environment is just a mere reflection of your inside self. Whatever you think of yourself will be reflected on your outside world.

Most people think that having a good and secure job will lead them to riches. But unfortunately, it has been proven wrong by many parents today. But the saddest part of it is that they don't even understand why after spending their lives for the company that they are serving, they retire broke. They blame the government for not setting a much higher minimum wage scale and for implementing huge taxes. But they fail to look at themselves as the cause of their financial failures.

Poor people's practice is this: whenever they receive their salary, the first thing they do is spend it on everything they think is necessary. They pay their tax, pay their bills, pay debt and then take some for their leisure, and then if there's something left over, then they save it. More often than not there is nothing left to save. That is their formula of success:

Income-Expenses = Savings.

Unfortunately, if their expenses are much greater than their income then the result instead of savings is debts. Is that true? Yes! Ask those people who spend their wants thru the credit card. Before they receive their income it was already literally spent before their pay day. Ask those parents whose habit was to line up with anybody or any institution available which offered loans even if they knew that they did not have enough money to pay for it.

Most of us envy people who have salaries of P50,000 pesos or more a month. But as long as their formula in handling their money is "Income-Expenses = Savings" they are still poor! Generally, if you belong to the group whose mere source of income is your job then you are poor. That is why they called JOB as Just Over Broke; living your life from pay check to pay check and at the end of the month with no money. You don't even know until when your job will last. And by the time you retire you will beg from your children or your siblings to take care of you.

Whenever you offer an investment opportunity to poor people their first reaction is negative for they presume that any investment is risky. But they never thought that spending all their money and not thinking for the future is not just risky but financial stupidity as well.

LEVEL 2-ORDINARY PEOPLE

FORMULA NO.2:
INCOME-SAVINGS = EXPENSE

This formula is the teaching of our great grandparents. During their time, people who practiced this dogma become rich. Those were the days that job security was a known practice. Whatever they earned with their high paying job, they saved it and bought assets later. They kept their daytime job, kept on saving, buying assets and when they retire, the company that they served will take care of them, including their health care insurance.

Today, this is no longer applicable. Unfortunately, there are still a lot of financial planners that teach this concept. The "Income-Saving = Expense" formula is a thing of the past. According to Robert Kiyosaki on his book Rich Dad Poor Dad, nowadays, savers are losers.

True enough, when was the last time you checked your savings account passbook? Did you see how much interest income are you receiving on your savings account? Before it was good to save, banks were paying very attractive interests, but today the average interest rates of banks on savings account is 1% not inclusive of the 20% tax. Then consider the inflation rate (the decrease in purchasing power of money] which averages to 6%.

I often hear "I'd rather put my money in the bank with a guarantee that I could have it anytime I need, than to put it in such a risky investment."

Even without tax, your money is already losing 5% value compounded annually, so every time you save, it means it guaranties only one thing—your losses.

The major concern of most savers why they put it in savings account is safety for their money. This is not always true for how many times have you heard about banks that closed down and was never able to return the money of their depositors. I have seen market vendors and other ordinary people crying in front of the bank that just declared bankruptcy, begging to give them back their hard earned money that they saved for their children's education.

But don't get me wrong, there is a logical explanation why you need to save in the bank, like putting it in there as your back-up fund or budget fund, but never as your investment in a savings account.

I must admit that it is better to save your money, than to spend it all and leave nothing for the future. My suggestion to you is that if you are this kind of person, don't be sad for this is just the beginning of your much sophisticated financial future. Just don't close your mind to other financial opportunities that will come. Make sure that whatever you save must later be put on investment or at least a part of it.

Invest in your education; learn how rich people grow their money. Learn what the rich people's formula on money is and with that the risk that you fear most will be lessened if not totally gone.

LEVEL 3-RICH PEOPLE

FORMULA NO.3:
INCOME-INVESTMENT = EXPENSE

This is now the formula of the rich people:

Income-Investment = Expense

Due to the ever increasing trend of inflation—the increase of prices of all commodities and the decrease of money's purchasing power, if you just saved your money as we have discussed, it will soon lose its value. So never save your money but instead invest it. And not just invest; you have to make sure that your investment return should be much greater than the inflation rate. Your goal in investing should be to beat inflation.

Investing your money is the primary means of expanding your wealth. Through this, you can turn your money into something bigger than it was before. Why then are ordinary people afraid to invest? Because most of them are driven by fear, they let their fear stop them to become rich.

Remember that fear is a natural instinct of a human being; it serves as an alarm warning that danger is approaching. That's how the primitive man survived during the early age, fear alarms them that another living form is about to eat them. So their instinct was to cover themselves or climb up the tree for protection.

It means all of us have fear; young, old, man, woman, poor and yes even rich people have fear. But the difference between the poor and the rich is that poor people let their fear stop them while rich people use their fear to drive them out of their comfort zone and lead them to become mighty rich than ever before.

Because of fear, whenever they receive money poor people spend it all (formula #1), for they believe that it's better to spend it by themselves than to lose it by investing since it is other people who would devour their money. With that in their minds, they find themselves with no money in the end.

There are two practices of investing that always cause a heated debate—diversification and focus. Focus means investing your money into a very profitable venture that will make you rich or gain a huge amount in the fastest way in your specialized investment vehicle. While diversification means putting your money into different classes of asset available. It follows the old notion that you don't put all your eggs in one basket.

The question now is which among them is the right one for you? Don't be fooled by them, there is no such thing as a right or wrong investment, only the wrong mindset of the investor. Don't discount any of them, for both of these practices have already delivered profitable results in the past.

Focus investing strategy in my opinion is a very wise one, if—and only if you have done your homework. Again we are back to the importance of financial education. If you want to focus your money in one venture that promises a very good fortune, then get all available education for that one and seek the help of a good mentor.

Focus investing is also easier to handle, for you have to concentrate on one or two classes of asset investments only, which is why it is called focus. For example you want to focus in investing in realty; you must ask yourself what kind of realty investment—housing, land, rentals, building, or commercial. Study the area you want to invest in. Then be an expert investor on that vehicle. If you want to focus on paper asset investment there are a lot to choose from: bonds, notes, stock. If you want stocks then ask yourself what kind of stock investment you want: small capital, big capital, growth, value and so on.

I met a realty investor at one time; he was a seaman before, a radio operator to be exact. But due to the effect of digital technology, radio operators became obsolete in modern shipping. A radio operator on board the ship is the communication officer; they are the ones who send and receive communication, either routine, urgent and especially distress messages. So that's how important they were before. But when the era of digital communication came, the complicated equipment that required one room to hold, can now be compressed into one computer and their intricate operation can now be done by regular mates on board the ship.

After losing his job as radio operator he and his wife started a business in realty by buying old houses in Sampaloc, Manila and then build buildings for boarding houses and re-selling it. They literally become millionaires in fastest time than they have imagined. They invested all the savings they accumulated during his sea going career and it made them instant millionaires. That is a good example of focus investing strategy.

The second strategy is diversification. This is the medium risk way of investing your money. Why medium, for I didn't want to say it was risk free, for there is no such thing as a risk free investment. You must understand that all investments have an associated risk.

Risk and return is directly proportional to each other; the bigger the risk the higher the return or the lower the risk the lower the return.

Unlike focus investing, if one of your business ventures did not become so profitable or at worst becomes a failure, you still have the opportunity to earn on your other investments. Like in our example above, if his venture with realty did not give him a very good return what would have happened to his savings?—gone!

With diversification, even if some of your other investment did not give you a very promising result you can still compensate it with your other profitable businesses. If you are a risk-averse person you will gain much if you diversify your investment. For most of risk-averse persons, they just put their money in vehicles that they believe to be safe but offers very limited gain. Look at the following table for comparison.

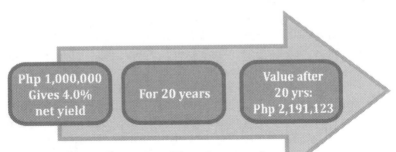

Table 6.1 Illustration of Focus Investments

Capital	Assumed Net Yield	Value After 20 yrs
Php 200,000	-100%	0
Php 200,000	0%	Php 200,000
Php 200,000	4%	Php 438,225
Php 200,000	8%	Php 932,191
Php 200,000	12%	Php 1.929,259
Total Net Gain	**Php 3,499,675**	

Table 6.2 Diversification of Investments

164

The above table is an example of two investment strategies that gave a difference of P 1,308,552. On the first example, the conservative investor placed his money in a long term horizon of 20 years that guaranteed a 4% net yield. Yes he doesn't lose any of his capital, but what he loses is an opportunity for his money to earn more.

In the second example the investor diversified his investment, dividing into P 200,000 each which was invested into five different classes of investments.

His first investment is not very fortunate, he lost everything after 20 years including his capital. The second one was not a very promising investment too, he didn't gain anything so after 20 year his P 200,000 remained to be P 200,000. His third investment had gained a meager income of 4% annually for 20 years which give him P 438,225. His fourth investment gave him 8% annually which resulted in P 932,191 after 20 years. And his highest gaining investment was the fifth one, which gave him 12% annually that resulted in P 1,929,259.

So what is the lesson of this comparison? It only means that if you are a conservative investor focusing your investments in ventures that guarantee return, it will not take you faster to your financial goal. The best way to manage your investment as a conservative should be diversification. While doing diversification, continue studying and learning the investments that you want to focus on, then after which you can follow the path of the previous seaman who became a millionaire by focusing his investment in realty. Focus investing is like specialization. Professional people who become specialists take a lot of advance studies like masterals or doctorate degrees before they earn their title as a specialist.

LEVEL 4-ABUNDANT PEOPLE

FORMULA NO.4:
INCOME-GIVING-INVESTMENT = EXPENSE

When you ask a person why he wants to be rich, the typical responses you will hear are:

"Because I want to have a beautiful and big house."
"Because I want to have a sports car—"yung" red."
"Because I want to travel around the world"

And a never ending list of wants . . . wants to own the world. That is the distinctive thinking of people who have a poor mentality and lives with a scarcity attitude. Again being poor is not how much money you have, but what attitude you have towards money.

When it comes to the arena of money there are two attitudes that compel people to do what is right, it becomes a source of motivation that mold their financial goal. They are the scarcity attitude and the abundant attitude.

Scarcity attitude is driven by fear and greed; they set their entire goals for nothing else but their personal gain. They always think that there is not enough for everybody, so their mind is set to always be a winner and in order for them to win somebody must lose. Unfortunately for this kind of person, even if he gains everything in this world it will never be enough, and most of them, died feeling empty and alone. So what is the meaning of money and success then?

While being in the state of abundance one is thinking that money has a deeper meaning and purpose. If you want to be in a state of abundance you must be rich not only from the outside but most importantly from the inside. Again, I will say, your outside world is just a mere reflection of your inner world. Abundant people think that being truly rich is like standing in a room that is full of different mirrors that whoever you are and whatever you have is reflected lavishly. They believe in giving back whatever they have. For they believe that it does not only multiply but magnify as well.

Therefore the abundant person uses a much advanced and sophisticated wealth formula which is:

Income-Giving-Investment = Expense

People living with this principle make sure that whenever they receive their income they first give at least 10% to the church and a charity they believe in, or to the Divine Being who gives them wealth. Then after which they invest at least another 10% portion of their income before they spend for their wants. They budget all their expenses based on their 80% income. Ask them if they feel worried with their finances they'll answer: No! Because money matters is all that is in your head, even if you earn a huge amount of money it will never be enough if you have the scarcity attitude.

Some say how can I live on the 80% of my meager income? I'm telling you that it's not the amount of money you have. The reason why you can't give is because of your attitude. What is the guarantee that you can give if your money became bigger? You'll feel greedier about it and the more you have the more you will question the miracle of giving.

Some people prefer to call it tithing. I am not being religious here, but believe me that whatever your faith is, giving is a universal law of abundance that every faith teaches. If it's hard for you to give your tithe when you have a small amount of money, then it will be tenfold harder when you have more.

Going back to the news article and discussed in the previous chapter, it was amazing how the 20 US billionaires encouraged each other to pledge half of their net worth to charity, it includes former richest man in the world Bill Gates (Owner of Microsoft], together with Warren Buffet (Owner of Berkshire Hataway], New York City Mayor Michael Bloomberg, Ted Turner (Owner of CNN] and another media mogul Barry Diller, "Star Wars" movie maker George Lucas and energy tycoon T. Boone Pickens. Totally there were 40 billionaires who have taken the pledge that would amount to 150 US Billion Dollars to be given away.

Bill Gates alone has a net worth of 53 Billion US Dollar and Warren Buffet has 47 Billion US Dollar. They promised to give half of their fortune to the people that they don't even know. That is what we call an abundant mentality. They don't just live with the 80% of their income but they challenged themselves to be happy with 50% of all they have, while most of us who has a very little money find it so hard to give away 10% of our income.

If you can't give P2,500 in your church or charity what more P25 Billion if you've become rich. Have you considered that maybe that's the very reason why God doesn't bless you with the money you want, because you are only thinking of yourself?

The secret of becoming truly rich is not owning the wealth of the world, but earning more than what you can in the best that you can so that you can help in the best possible way you can.

Do you have your goal at this point of time? If none, allow me to give you a very simple goal that will make you truly rich and successful. How about setting a goal to give 1 Million Pesos every year to charity and to your church? If you are practicing formula no.4, which is giving 10% before investing and spending, and you set a goal to give away 1 million every year, it means you are setting a goal to earning 10 million pesos every year.

The moment you experience the great blessing and miracle of abundance mentality—of giving away, try to set a much higher goal next time. Let's say that next year instead of giving 10%, give 20%, and then increase your giving attitude once you have reached every goal. Until such time you come to the point that you have the courage to give away half of what you own just like what the US billionaires pledged.

A friend of mine once asked me, "If what you are saying is true then why is one of my friends who practices tithing in his church still remain poor and problematic about money?"

If you are going to give, ask yourself how do you really feel about it? Do you feel happy or feel lousy when you are giving the money away? If you feel that something is holding you back, then maybe your heart is not in it, that you have bad feelings about giving. For sure nobody wants to attract bad feelings in their lives and with that you probably won't attract more money too.

Give only if you feel good about it with little or no expectation that it will come back to you. The moment you detach yourself from scarcity mentality, abundance will start to move in and take its place. Giving leads to receiving that leads to more wealth. Give for the essence of giving.

Do you know what my greatest goal is? To reverse my giving, right now I'm trying my best to give 10% of what I'm earning but one day I wish I will come to the point that I could give 90% and live in 10% of what I have. Just Imagine if those group of US billionaires will come to the point that they could give their 90% and just live with their 10% what will be their net worth by then.

It was said that William Colgate, the founder of the Colgate Palmolive Empire was one such giver with an enormous abundance mentality. His faith in God led him to tithe 10% on his income, when his business prospered he made an additional pledge that by the end of his life, it was rumoured that he was already giving back 90% of his income. With the size of his company at the time of his death, you can assume how much he must have been earning. Someone once said that "we can never outgive God".

So don't aim for having a simple wealth, but aim for greater wealth, for if that happens, you can have much greater opportunities to help others. Aim to have a multi billion peso and the moment you reach that goal give it all away. For what is important is not the money that you have acquired but the person you have become. After that we can prove to the world that money is not the root of all evil but it is the LOVE OF MONEY that is the root of all evil.

WEALTH CALCULATOR

Everyone who dreams of becoming rich, doesn't start their month planning on how to squander their fortune. But unfortunately this is not what is happening in the real world. Everybody wants to be rich and enjoy spending at the same time. Whenever I give suggestions on how to save a little everyday so that at the end of the month they could have P10,000 to invest, most of them are uninterested. So this time let's reverse the process. What does it take to squander P10,000 a month? By simply spending P333 everyday! That's how simple it is to flush your money down the drain.

List down all your expenses everyday in one notebook and you will find that actually you are spending an average of more than P333 a day on things that are not really important. How many bottled iced tea and fruit juices or soft drinks do you consume every day? How much do you spend per value meal every time you dine out in a fast food restaurant? How many sticks of cigarette do you smoke to burn your lungs and destroy your health and the health of those around you? And how much money do you spend every Friday or Saturday night with your barkada along Malate, Makati, The Fort or Libis? Maybe right now you're thinking that P10,000 is not really enough for all those unnecessary things, that you don't realize that it costs you your most important goal. Yes, you need to unwind after a hard day's work, but you don't need to do it in the expense of selling your future for today's whims and caprices.

Like my colleague named Francisco, he's working in one of the offices in Makati and earning P35,000 a month. When I explained to him how he can be a millionaire in the soonest time by investing at least 10% of his income, he gave all possible objections that he can come up with. Then when we dug deeper on his excuses, we found out that a majority of his income goes to his extravagant lifestyle.

When we were young I knew Francisco as the simplest guy in our group. So I was stunned to learn the big changes that happened to him. After a couple of hours listening, I discovered that the reason was he spent most of his salary was just to cope up with the pressure among his officemates.

That kind of situation happens everywhere. I've seen a lot of that even on board our ship. Why let others rule your life? Keep your priorities in mind and stay focused. Remember every peso you spend will cost you a thousand pesos of your financial independence.

Daily Savings	Monthly Savings	Rate of Return	10 yrs	20 yrs	30 yrs
33	1,000	4%	147,250.00	366,770.00	694,050.00
		12%	247,855.00	980,385.00	3,255,511.00
67	2,000	4%	294,500.00	733,550.00	1,388,100.00
		12%	495,710.00	1,960,770.00	6,511,023.00
100	3,000	4%	441,750.00	1,100,320.00	2,082,150.00
		12%	743,565.00	2,941,154.00	9,766,534.00
167	5,000	4%	736,250.00	1,833,870.00	3,470,250.00
		12%	1,239,275.00	4,901,924.00	16,277,556.00
233	7,000	4%	1,030,750.00	2,567,420.00	4,858,350.00
		12%	1,734,985.00	6,862,694.00	22,788,579.00
267	8,000	4%	1,178,000.00	2,934,2000.00	5,552,400.00
		12%	1,982,000.00	7,843,078.00	26,044,090.00
300	9,000	4%	1,325,250.00	3,300,960.00	6,246,450.00
		12%	2,230,695.00	8,823,462.00	29,299,602.00
333	10,000	4%	1,472,500.00	3,667,750.00	6,940,490.00
		12%	2,478,550.00	9,803,848.00	32,555,113.00
500	15,000	4%	2,208,750.00	5,501,610.00	10,410,750.00
		12%	3,717,825.00	14,705,772.00	48,832,668.00
667	20,000	4%	2,945,000.00	7,335,500.00	13,880,980.00
		12%	4,957,100.00	19,607,697.00	65,110,226.00

Table 6.3 Table of Wealth Calculator

THE RAT RACE

"The trouble with the rat-race is that even if you win, you're still a rat."
Lily Tomlin

When I was just a kid, my daily habit was to daydream. Especially when the weather was cold like during rainy days, I would just lie down at the corner of our "papag" (a bed made of wood] and hug my pillow. I felt elated every time I was out of the real world, dreaming that I was living in a very big mansion with full of servants. Eating sumptuous food and having a lot of toys all around my house.

Though I must admit that there are times in my life that I wanted to give up, for all my life, all I did was to work, work and work. When I was just a kid, I've experienced a lot of jobs like working in a factory together with my mother and selling everything and anything that my neighbors would ask me to sell for a few centavos commission.

Then when I was in college, I worked in one of the biggest food chains in the country to support my education. By then I noticed that my day dreaming started to fade away. I forgot about my habit of daydreaming. I started to accept that maybe life will be hard for me all the time, that no matter what effort I do, I can never change my miserable life.

Despite my ability to earn a little more than what I was earning before, I felt that my life was becoming more complicated and lonely compared in those days that we were just living for what the day could offer. Now I come to realize that the major reason of my loneliness is because I stopped dreaming—fantasizing that I was living in a rich world.

I'm sure that this is true for everybody. We tend to forget how to dream for all of us become too busy keeping with the rat race of life. We start our day by waking up very early in the morning even if we don't want to, but because we have to, or else we don't have the money at the end of the month to pay our bills and buy food for our family. We go home late in the evening exhausted, enduring the traffic and missing dinner with the kids. Even if you want to help your kids with their home work, your energy will not allow it anymore. We end our day worrying for the next day's battle.

For us OFW's we have to spend a year or more away from our family and work like slaves in return for the dollars to bring home at the end of our contract. Some risk their lives in a foreign land or in vicious seas, especially for seamen like me, just so we can provide a much better way of living for our family.

Try to remember the day you graduated from college. A mixed emotion of fear and joy filled your heart. You are happy because you have graduated but on the other hand you are also fearful for now is time to find a job. Not because you love to, but that is what people around us expect us to do.

In fact if you rest too long after graduation, people will start to criticize you that sometimes they will even push you to apply for a job that is not even related to what you have studied. Look around and see how many young graduates of Nautical and Marine Engineering [my field of profession] ended up being security guards. Yes it's sad but that is the reality, I really feel sorry for them. I don't criticize security guards posted outside banks and business establishments keeping the businesses safe, as long as it is the dream they want to achieve after studying in college for four years.

In the same manner, how many graduates of various courses like engineering, accounting, nursing and so on, end up being a call center agents, speaking in fancy American or English accents talking with people from the other side of the world. The biggest question now is whether it was the failure of their parents or a failure of the education system that we have?

After keeping their jobs for ten or even twenty years, how many have become financially independent? After staying a couple of years in your job, how happy have you become? Are you seeing a brighter future or are you just letting chances bring you to wherever they want you to drift to? These are questions that most of us try to avoid, because the majority of us don't have an answer at hand. But have you ever considered that maybe we have to control our financial lives so that we can enjoy life the way we want to live?

Table 6.4 The Rat Race

Refer to Figure 6.4 and let's try to take a look at a typical employee's life. The moment they receive their salary, the government will automatically take its share of what they have worked hard for—the tax. Then they need to pay bills to keep afloat—electricity, water, telephone, cable TV subscription, etc; pay off debts that are either personal loans, housing loans or a car loan. Then they'll try to enjoy a lifestyle which other people enjoy: they'll go to the malls, buy things that would make them feel secure even for a moment, amidst their financial insecurity,. Then before the month ends, or even just before the middle of the month, they end up with no more money. They then become impatient for the next payday and when it comes, the same routine will occur again, and again month after month.

If this is your lifestyle, even if you get promoted every year and your salary increased every year, what is the chance that you will become financially independent? While your salary may increase, your taxes, bills, debts and lifestyle will also increase and oftentimes much faster than your salary. For sure every end of the month you will have no money.

I have seen a lot of this with OFWs, seamen in particular; they started as ordinary seaman with the enough salary. Then got promoted to the next higher position as able bodied seaman, salary is still enough. Then took a license to be an officer, just the same—salary is just enough. Until they become a Captain of the ship, guess what?—salary is still just enough!

PAYING YOURSELF FIRST

A humorous motivational speaker, Zig Ziglar once said, "Money is not that important but it ranks next to oxygen". If that's how important money is, then why give it to other people by spending it on things that are not important. If money is important to make life worth living, at least comfortably, wouldn't it be a good idea to spend it on things which is of equal importance in value? And what is that important thing which has great value?—YOU! With this, we have to pay ourselves first before we pay other people. Now how do we pay ourselves first?

Are you paying MERALCO or other power utility companies for your electricity? How about water utilities? SMART, Globe, Talk n' Text, or Sun for your telecom needs? What about Jollibee, Mcdo and other fast food chains? Starbucks? San Miguel Beer, San Mig Light, Red Horse or any other alcoholic beverages? Are you paying them every month? How about to Mr. Henry Sy of SM or Mr. Gokongwei of Robinson's, are you paying them every month? I'm sure you are!

But what about the person called—YOU, who is working all his life, that even if he doesn't want to go to work because he's feeling sick and he still has to, or else he'll will lose his job? It's YOU—you who is constantly nagged by your boss. You—who can't even attend the PTA meeting of your children because you have a work schedule; how much are you paying for yourself?

Question: If you get sick, injured or have a critical illness, can you approach those businessmen that you've paid first, and ask them to take care of you because you've already given them your money? None of them will bother. You have to accept that, and I'm sure you know that. When you get old and are about to retire with no money; can you ask them to adopt you because you have helped them in their businesses instead of planning for your own retirement? OF COURSE NOT!

While explaining this in one of my seminars, one attendees told me "But we have to pay MERALCO or else we will not have electricity the following day . . ."

Yes, indeed you have to pay them, I replied. I then told him about two men, one was paying P8,000 and the other only P2500 a month for their electricity bills. How much was the difference between the two? That's a huge P5,500 difference. And if you ask the first man to invest, he will tell you that it will not fit in his budget.

Now think, if he invests even P5,000 monthly in an investment vehicle that would give him a rate of return of at least an average of 12% compounded annually. He will have had P1,239,275 in ten years or P4,901,924 in twenty years. That was just by paying himself first. After explaining that to them, the guy sat quietly and nod his head in agreement.

In our financial life, we have what we call our present income. That present income is intended to be used for our present needs. Then we also have our future income; income that we expect to receive in the future, but we still have to work for that. That future income is intended to be used for future needs.

The common mistake committed by most people is that they use their future income for their present needs or wants. For example, you use your credit card without even thinking of your ability to pay and just keep your fingers crossed that by the end of the month you will still have your paycheck. The question is: is your future income guaranteed?—NO! How about future need?—YES! So never use your future income for your present needs or wants. Learn to live on what you have.

So the question now is how do you pay yourself first? Take control of your personal finances; do not succumb to the temptation of giving in to peer pressure. Every time you receive your salary or present income, set aside a portion of it regularly, let's say 10% of it. Then invest that 10% in an investment vehicle that you fully understand. So that even if your future income will not come, like in the event of a job lay off, business bankruptcy or other similar set back, you'd still have something to use for your future needs.

WANT VS. NEED

"There are two ways of being happy: We must either diminish our wants or augment our means-either may do-the result is the same and it is for each man to decide for himself and to do that which happens to be easier."
Benjamin Franklin

Wanting and needing are two different things and it is often confused by a lot of people. I know of many who always use the line "At least I've spent my money on the most important things in life like food and clothing . . ."

We were taught in school the basic needs of man are food, clothing, shelter and education But most people find it difficult to differentiate their basic needs from their wants. Yes we need food, but it does not mean eating at a fast food restaurant every day. We need clothing but it does not mean having expensive signature clothes all the time. And worse, we even perceive that keeping up with our friends and neighbors as being the way to be accepted by the society where we belong as a need.

What is wrong with eating in a fancy restaurant, wearing a signature clothing or buying new gadgets available in the market? Actually, that in itself, nothing, in fact our life's goal is to live comfortably. But what makes it wrong is sacrificing the more important things in your life for the short term pleasure of buying those things which are not so important.

In my case, my life's dream is to own and drive a BMW car, but that can wait for seven to ten years as per to my life's goal. I also believe that it is good for us to want for things that only a few elite people can afford, for that will serve as the spice and inspiration of our life.

I'm not saying that it's wrong to have expensive and fancy things. In fact, I always push others to dream for these things so that at least before they leave this world, they can experience owning one if not all of them. But you must know what your priority is and not sacrifice the things that matter most with the things that matter least. If at the moment you think you can't afford to have those fancy things, don't stop there and say "I can't afford it" but instead ask yourself what can you do to have it, but not at the expense of the more important things.

How do we determine if what we are buying is a want or a need? The best way to differentiate the two is whenever you see something that you'd like to buy, ask yourself, "If I don't buy it now, would I still be able to live without it or not?" If the answer is no, then that is a need, so buy it. But if the honest answer is yes, then hold that thing and enjoy it. While holding it, feel as if you own it, then after a while put it back carefully in its display rack for surely it is just a want. You have enjoyed the moment of having it for a while and yet you still have your money when you leave the store.

Look around your house; open your closet, drawers, and cabinets. How many of the things that you own today, you don't even remember the reason why you bought it in the first place. How many of the clothes that fill your packed closet you have used only once? Maybe it was only during the Christmas party of your company, or worse some of them you have not ever used yet.

According to Warren Buffet, "if you buy things that you don't need you'll soon sell things that you need". If you fail to set aside for your back-up fund because you always bought things to feed your wants, when a real emergency occurs, you might even sell the house you are currently living in. Don't fool yourself by thinking that every day is a sunny day, that rainy days will never come.

One way to control yourself in spending your hard earned money on trivial things is by keeping a daily record of your expenses. You must know where your money goes or else you'll wake up one day penniless and wondering who robbed you of your fortune. The truth is when you don't track where your money goes, it's too easy to overspend and make yourself believe that there is a continuous flow of money every day.

Studies show that those people who are on a diet program make more progress if they keep a diet journal or a list of what they eat every day. A person who wants to be financially independent will have the same effect if he/she devotedly lists all his/her expenses.

You can use "Table 6.3 My Daily Expenses Table" that I usually give to my clients. You can modify the names or categories of each expense depending on what is applicable to you. This will help you know how much money you spent and where you spent it. At the end of the month, analyze how much you spent on each category.

At the end of the month, after completing your expenses table, evaluate your expenses [Table 6.5]. Typical companies do a monthly evaluation of their expenses to make sure that their company will stay ahead all the time. So why can't we be more concerned with our own life, after all it is far more important than the company we work for.

THIS IS WHERE MY MONEY GOES

	Associa-tion Dues	Car Main-tenance	Car Pay-ments	Charity	Clothing	Com-muting	Dining Out	Educa-tion	Food/ Grocer-ies	Gasoline	Gifts	Health Care	Hobbies	Insu-rance	House Keeping	Insur-ance	Personal Items	Property Taxes	Recrea-tion	Rent or Mort-gage	Subscrip-tions	Utilities	Vacations	Others	Total
1																									
2																									
3																									
4																									
5																									
6																									
7																									
8																									
9																									
10																									
11																									
12																									
13																									
14																									
15																									
16																									
17																									
18																									
19																									
20																									
21																									
22																									
23																									
24																									
25																									
26																									
27																									
28																									
29																									
30																									
31																									
Total																									

Table 6.5 My Daily Expense Table

EVALUATION			
Where Can I Cut Back?	**Target Cut On Budget**	**What Cheaper Alternatives Can I Find?**	**If Cut Back is Successful, Add to My Goal**

Table 6.6 Evaluation form of monthly Expenses

For example, at the end of the month you realize that you've spent P25,000 in dining out alone, why not make a target to cut down at least 25% of it, which is P6,250. You see, I'm not even asking you to stop dining out but to at least to cut it down. Find a cheaper alternative like being home early to have dinner with your family. With that, you not only save P6,250 but also strengthen your family relationships by being with them. How about bringing packed lunch to your work place? It's not only cheap but healthy as well.

Imagine if you will be successful in saving P6,250 for the next 20 years and invest those savings in a mutual fund, lets say it gives you an average of 15% rate of return, you will have P7,452,770 net of charge at the end of 20 years! Now tell me, do you think that being rich is still impossible? And that's your savings when you minimize only your dining out. There are still a lot more you can save from your other expenses that are not usually important.

YOUR HUMAN ECONOMIC VALUE

"Your net worth to the world is usually determined by what remains after your bad habits are subtracted from your good ones."
Sidney Madwed

How do things become so valuable? There are three factors to consider: it is highly important, it is rare, and it is beautiful. But most people overlook all these three factors and forget that they are endowed to us by the time we emerged into this world. The scriptures say, "We are the caretakers of God's creation". All of us are created as a unique individual. Meaning, however you search the world there is only one you, that's how rare we are. And we are beautiful for God created us from his own image, unless you want to believe that you came from the image of monkeys.

It's sad to see that a lot of people miss the fact on how valuable each of us are and easily forget to increase or even maintain that value. This is true even when we handle our finances; we don't care so much because we don't know what our worth is. In a financial aspect, we can define our own human economic value in terms of our Net Worth.

Like managing a business, finding your net worth is very crucial to the success or failure of your life. Net worth simply means the total of your entire asset minus your liabilities. Knowing your net worth is a big help for you to measure your financial progress from year to year or even month to month.

I have a shipmate named Jimmy, He's a 2nd officer and we've sailed on the same ship twice. After attending my series of seminars on financial planning, I helped in assessing his financial standing. After making a full inventory of his assets and liabilities, he surprised himself to find out that after working so long aboard ship and building some small businesses, he had a net worth of almost seven million pesos.

That was the only time he was able to fully appreciate the entire endeavor he had made. By living frugally, he was able to buy agricultural land and build businesses on agri-farming. For him to know the progress of his business; I taught him how to calculate his net worth. He was so thankful that for the first time he was truly sure that what he was doing would bring him his life's desire.

That's how important net worth is. Have a goal that each year you should have a growth and continuously monitor it. I assure you that the percentage of your growth on your net worth will be more rewarding than the figure of your income.

Finding your net worth is easy. You only need to make an inventory of what you own and what you owe. Here's how:

1] List all your tangible assets. This would be your house, real estate (if any] your car etc. Put an estimate on their current market value. Remember, houses and cars depreciate, it's your real estate properties (land, lot)that appreciates depending on their locations.

2] Next, gather the latest statements of account of all your liquid assets. This includes your checking and savings accounts and your certificate of deposits. If you have money in the money market fund and/or treasury bill etc, that should be included, too. Even the cash value of your life insurance policy as well (you can find that in your policy contract].

3] If you are good in taking care of your money and have started investing to make it work for you, congratulations!

MY BALANCE SHEET
My Net Worth As of _____

ASSETS		LIABILITIES	
Personal Investments		Personal Loans	_____
Residence [House & Lot]	_____	Car Loans	_____
Collectibles/ Art/Antiques	_____	Home Mortgage	_____
Car	_____	Life Insurance Policy Loan	_____
Home Furnishings	_____	Income Tax Liability	_____
Jewelry	_____	Business Loan	_____
Other Assets	_____	Credit Card	_____
TOTAL	_____	**TOTAL**	_____

Liquid Assets

Checking Accounts	_____
Savings Accounts	_____
Time Deposits	_____
Money Market Accounts	_____
Treasury Bills	_____
Cash Value of Life Ins.	_____
TOTAL	_____

MY NET WORTH _____

Investments

Stocks	_____
Bonds	_____
Mutual Funds	_____
Business Net Worth	_____
TOTAL	_____

Retirement Funds

Pension (Present Lump Sum Value]	_____
PagIbig Funds	_____
Company Retirement Acct.	_____
TOTAL	_____

MY TOTAL ASSETS _____

6.4 My Balance Sheet

Now list all your investment accounts and its current account values; like stocks, bonds, mutual fund, or if you have a business; know how much your asset with it.

4] Then review all your retirement fund account, like Pag-ibig fund, pension plan or company retirement account.

5] Add the value of all your assets that you have listed and that represent your total assets.

6] At this point you have to make an inventory of your liabilities such as car loan, balance on your mortgage of your house. As well as your personal liabilities like personal loan, credit card, loan on your insurance policy and other debt that you may have.

7] Sum up all your liabilities and get the total.

8] Then to get your net worth just subtract your total liabilities from your total assets.

Use the following form I've provided to calculate your net worth. Don't worry for now, no matter how small or big it is, even if it is negative, this is just your starting point.

After completing your first balance sheet, set a date when you are going to repeat the process in making another one. Ideally it should be every three months or quarterly so that you can appreciate the progress you are making.

Don't be concerned with the amount of your income. No matter how big your income is, it is useless if you don't know the growth of your net worth. The same is true even if your current income today is small because if your net worth is increasing every year, it only means that you are on the right track to riches.

How do you increase your net worth? There are several ways to do it. First is, you can increase your income by having another job. Or second, you must regularly keep a part of your present income, let's say 10% of it, then invest the money that you've saved then reinvest its interest. And the last one is by living within your means. Not necessarily below your means—enjoy your life, but don't spend more than what you earn.

Rich and successful people are concerned with their growth in all aspects of their lives, and yes, even with their net worth. So if you want to become one of them, start focusing your financial goal on your net worth. To appreciate more the difference between net worth and income consider this example:

Let's say you built your own business in the year 2002, and that you earned P500,000 that year. Here's what happened to your company after that year with the income of your business:

YEAR	ANNUAL INCOME
2002	500,000
2003	950,000
2004	1,171,000
2005	2,907,000
2006	4,651,200
2007	6,976,800
2008	9,767,776
2009	12,697,776
2010	15,237,331

I asked a lot of people what they think of this company's financial situation if they are the owner of it. The majority of them said that they would be very happy for they have millions of pesos every year.

"After eight years the income of my company has become 15.2 million. Isn't that great?"

That's how naïve your thinking is if you don't understand the growth of your net worth. Always figure your growth in percentages not by the actual amount you earn every year. For example, if your income this year is P50,000, then the following year it becomes P100,000, that would great for then you have a 100% increase in your growth (100,000-50,000 = 50,000/50,000

= 1.0]. But lets say that after earning P100,000, the following year your income became P150,000, is that good? No, because that's 50% decline in your income (150,000-100,000 = 50,000/100,000 = 0.50]! For you to maintain your 100% you must earn P200,000.

Now using my previous example, let's take the percentage of the growth of your company you have built.

YEAR	ANNUAL INCOME	GROWTH OF NET WORTH
2002	500,000	-
2003	950,000	90%
2004	1,171,000	80%
2005	2,907,000	70%
2006	4,651,200	60%
2007	6,976,800	50%
2008	9,767,776	40%
2009	12,697,776	30%
2010	15,237,331	20%

Justification:

Ex: 950,000-500,000 = 450,000
       450,000 / 500,000 = 0.9 or 90%

The table looks deceivingly good since we are receiving millions of pesos every year. But after determining the growth, the real story reveals that your company is actually losing 10% every year on its growth. If you didn't know that, it's so unfortunate for unknowingly you let it happen for the past eight years.

So how can you invite your friends or other people to invest in your business? Will you tell them that they will lose 10% every year on the value of their money?

So now you know why rich people are very particular with the percentage of their growth annually and very worried once there is no growth and very much worried when it is declining. But most ordinary people are just happy to receive an annual income of the same amount year after year, which is 0% growth! If you consider the effects of inflation, it would become not just zero but a loss that is compounded year after year.

This is the justification of the saying that we cannot be rich by just being an employee in our entire life. Rich and successful people became very rich by embarking on the risk of building their own business and constantly focusing their goal on the growth of their net worth.

But if you think you are not yet ready to build your own business at least make sure that you are constantly keeping a part of your salary and investing it to increase your net worth.

Knowing the importance of net worth will keep you out of being envious of your manager's salary. If you know how to increase your net worth and he or she doesn't know it, chances are, you will become a millionaire ahead of them, even if you are holding the lowest position in your company. I have seen it many times among seamen; an ordinary seaman becomes a millionaire faster than the Captain. The ordinary seaman built his own business then retired early. While the captain has to keep sailing until his retirement because he spent a majority of his income on liabilities.

WHO IS RICHER?

> *"Who is wise? He that learns from everyone.*
> *Who is powerful? He that governs his passions.*
> *Who is rich? He that is content. Who is that? Nobody."*
> **Benjamin Franklin**

The world defines wealth based on the abundance of material possessions a person has. We believe that rich people should dress rich, eat gourmet foods, drive luxury cars and have a name that sounds rich, in short—they should look rich and smell rich.

How wealthy should you be? Since one indicator of your wealth is your net worth, a person's income and his age should be the factor on how wealthy he should be. The more income you receive the higher your net worth should be. The longer you work on a high paying job then the greater your chance to accumulate much wealth. But thats the hypothetical situation, but the question is: "Is that what really happens?"

Once you understand the value of knowing your net worth, you will definitely see wealth in a different perspective. Remember that your wealth is not based on your worldly possessions and definitely not based on the income you receive. It is based on what you keep from what you have earned and increases its value. The true measure is how long can you live with what you have right now when you lose your income. It means that if you are asked to stop working, how long can you support your needs with the money you have without having to work again for the rest of your life. Let's look at three different situations:

Jose had a net worth of 2 million pesos when he lost his job due to mass lay off. The company that he was working for downsized because of bad economic conditions. How long can Jose live with his 2 million pesos is the real measure of his true wealth.

Since Jose was working as a Manager, his living expenses were high for he always tried to keep up with his neighbors who were of the middle class. If his monthly expenses costs around P100,000, it means that based on his net worth, Jose can only survive for 20 months.

The same fate happened to Michael, who was working at the same company as Jose with the same level of position but in a different department. Michael, just like Jose, also had a net worth of 2 million pesos. But unlike Jose his monthly expense was only P50,000. So, if ever Michael will not be able to find another job, he will be able to survive for 40 months.

Looking at Jose and Michael's situation side by side, who is richer between the two? Since we measure wealth on how long we can live with what we have, we could say that Michael is richer. Two people with same salary and position but different on how they spent their money—that difference is wealth. And we must remember that net worth is not necessarily a liquid asset, if your net worth is heavily skewed to your home equity, you have a bigger problem. What are you going to do if all your hard earned money went to your expensive house in a prime subdivision of middle class people or to your expensive car and you don't have investments in liquid assets like bonds, stocks, money market fund or mutual fund?

The third guy we have is Antonio, like Jose and Michael, he also worked for the same company. But unlike them, Antonio worked as a janitor. When the company's business got bad, Antonio was also one of those affected and he also lost his job.

But unlike Jose and Michael, Antonio only had a net worth of P300,00 and it was mostly on liquid assets for he invested in a cooperative investment program in his community. His total monthly expense was only P5,000. It means that Antonio can survive without working again for 60 months.

So, who is the richest among the three? This is how important it is for you to know that your wealth is not your salary, not your car or not even the beautiful house you own and live in. It is what you keep from what you are earning. Not because you are earning a huge salary and enjoy luxury things doesn't always mean you are rich. Maybe you are just "living high".

What if Antonio accumulated the same net worth same as with Jose and Michael? If Antonio was able to accumulate the same 2 million pesos and kept his expenses the same, then he can live for 400 months! That's almost 33 years without even working anymore.

Let's take a look at Alfred's case. He was an OFW working as an engineer in one of the biggest electronic company in the U.S. He is now 65 years old and was able to get retirement benefits totalling P10 million. Due to ignorance in financial planning, when he received his money, he bought a new house as his retirement house that cost P5 million. He then spent another P2 million for house improvements and bought a brand new car that cost him another P2 million. So how much was left for him?—P1 million! How long do you think Alfred can live on that little amount? For sure, that with his expensive way of living, his P1 million will be gone in less than a year.

One more real life situation, Jayson worked as CFO at one construction firm where his monthly salary was P150,000. His monthly expense was also P150,000 and there were times when it was more than that. Jayson is a happy-go-lucky person and had a gambling habit. Because of this, he was tempted to make an illegal transaction in his company and it was discovered after their annual audit. To cut a long story short, he lost his job. He tried hard to find another job that would give him the same amount of salary but couldn't due to what he did in his previous company.

One day he was able to find a new job in a small company but with a salary of only P30,000 monthly. Question: will Jayson be able to survive on his new salary? Definitely yes, if survival is the main issue. But why did he have to wait for the unfortunate thing to happen, to live his life in a P30,000 monthly salary? Imagine if he had a salary of P150,000 and lived on P30,000, it means he would have been able to invest P120,000 monthly that would have soon made him rich in a very short period of time. He didn't need to work anymore and didn't need to sell himself out for money.

As a saying goes "No one plans to fail . . . we only fail to plan." If you don't know what you want in life then how do you expect life can give you what you want. Don't wait for emergency situations to happen before you plan for it. This is the very reason why crews on board ships keep a regular "fire and abandon ship drill" for them to be prepared in a real emergency situation; to keep them from being caught off guard. It is much better if we consistently plan while things are easy so that when difficulties arise we will be prepared.

The simplest way to be rich is to understand how money works. The same is true about life, if you understand how it works you can use it to your advantage. The problem with most people is that we are trained and educated to work for the money but nobody teaches us on how money works.

Money works in a cyclic way, that's the reason they call it circulation of money—currency. It moves from one hand to another. Every time money moves into your hand, you are in the winning side, and every time money moves away from your hand, you are in the losing side.

For example after receiving your salary, you go to SM to spend everything; buy things you don't need and eat in a fancy restaurant inside the mall. In this case you are on the losing side, because money goes into your hand and immediately out as you pass it on to another hand; into the hand of Mr. Henry Sy and to say so, he's then on the winning side.

The simple secret to riches is you must always be on the winning side like Henry Sy and learn how to let the money grow while it is in your hands.

If you have a good plan and always take action based on it, there is no reason for you not to reach your goal or your wants in life. It is very important that you set a goal where to put all the money that you receive and will receive, for if you don't, then others will set goals to get your money. So stop being a loser.

Men and women who have accumulated great wealth in life are those who understood how life works by taking in and learning every lesson they could muster. They possessed indomitable willpower and the ability to persist and be triumphant until they achieve the success they want. The more you persist to be rich even when the going gets rough, the more self-discipline and mastery you tend to have and sure enough, there is no reason for you not to be rich.

DOUBLE YOUR MONEY

Just making money is not enough anymore.
Now we have to worry about our money making money.
Woody Allen, b. 1935
American film maker

There was a time that the pyramiding scam was booming in the Philippines. Double your money was the magic word that most of the uninformed investors were attracted to. Like moths being lured by the beauty of a lamp, a great number of people fell into the shining trap of the fad. It was so enticing to hear how your money will double at a very short period of time. Many, mostly ordinary Filipinos, succumbed to that tempting offer. I've heard of story after story of even retirees willing to risk their hard earned retirement savings, money they've allotted for their golden years, just so they can be rich immediately. Imagine yourself receiving huge amounts every month because the interest they offered was quite big.

Only a few realize that by having a right financial education, doubling your money is not that impossible at all without having to jump into the vortex of the pyramiding scam. For this to happen, you must take advantage on what we call compounded interest. We have mentioned compound interest many times in the previous topics. So what it is then?

Interest is the sum of money paid on your principal investment expressed in percentage, usually computed per year. It is your reward after taking the associated risk on the investment that you have taken part in. Theoretically, risk and interest is directly proportional; the higher the risk the higher the interest and vice versa. In some cases, interest is paid not only on the principal investment but as well as on the cumulative total of past interest payments. This process is what we call compounded interest.

To simplify, we may say that money is our slave and the reason why we invest our money is to make it work for us—to make our money be our slaves, not we being slaves to money. These slaves that we have will produce offspring (interest) in the long run. For you to take advantage of compounded interest, the offspring of your slaves must, in turn, also be your slaves and also their grand-grandchildren and so on. In the long run you will not notice that your original slave has already multiplied more than tenfold. That's how amazing compounded interest is.

The problem with money that we have is not the money per se, but the way we handle money. With this, compound interest may work with us or against us. How is that? If you use your money in investment, then compound interest will work for you. But once you use your money in spending things on credit, its a liability, then compounded interest will work against you.

Compounded interest works on credit cards and other credit instruments too. It also holds true if you get a loan from the bank. When you buy a car or a house on credit or even when you avail of a personal loan, interest payments are compounded too, more so if you have a default in payment.

How do we determine then, when our money has doubled? The Rule of 72 is a simple way to quickly estimate how long it will take for your money to be doubled. All you have to do is to determine the interest rate of your investment per year. If you don't have a fixed interest then averaging will give you a rough estimate.

To use the Rule of 72, simply divide 72 by the interest rate. The result is the number of years to make your money double with the prevailing interest rate. For example you place P100 in your savings account in the bank and it gives you 1% per annum. So, divide 72 by 1 and it will give you 72 also. It only means that in order for your P100 to become P200 it will take 72 years to double! Not to mention that you still have to pay a 20% tax on its earnings.

Now, if you think that to be safe is putting your money in the bank and enjoying 1% per annum will lead you to riches, think again. If you have that patience to wait for 72 year to double your money then good for you, but definitely not for me. The safety of our investment does not rely on the institution where we place our money, but on the mindset and education we have.

For you to double your money in the fastest rate, you must always consider the interest earning of your investment. And of course a full consideration of the risk involve and your risk appetite too. To know when your money will be doubled, here are some interest rates and the corresponding number of years to make it double:

With reference to our table above you can easily determine when your money will be doubled. So if somebody offers you an investment, you must ask first the following: What is the nature of business of the company you want to invest? What is the interest rate they will give you?

After knowing the interest rate, then just refer to our table, and you'll get the estimated year when it will be doubled.

INTEREST RATES	YEARS TO DOUBLE	INTEREST RATES	YEARS TO DOUBLE
1%	72	11%	6.5
2%	36	12%	6
3%	24	13%	5.5
4%	18	14%	5.1
5%	14	15%	4.8
6%	12	16%	4.5
7%	10.3	17%	4.2
8%	9	18%	4
9%	8	19%	3.8
10%	7.2	20%	3.6

Also with the Rule of 72 you can better understand the power of inflation. Taking the average long term inflation of our country, let's say 6%, it means that things that can be purchased at P100 today, after 12 years you will need P200 to buy or enjoy the same things or services. That's how important it is to constantly beat inflation whenever we invest our money.

HOLISTIC NATURE OF MONEY

> . . . Remember the Lord your God, for it is He who
> gives you the ability to produce wealth.
> **Deuteronomy 8:18**

I know a lot of seamen who wants to go into the money lending business. But some of them are being held back by the belief that it was evil to do such business. How many times have we heard that once you lend your money to somebody to earn interest and make some business, you will have "bukol" [lumps] all over your body. Some called it "gaba" (a Visayan term for curse], while some say its bad karma.

I'm not really sure how true that belief is. But I'm just wondering, why nobody has spread a belief that; once you borrow somebody's hard earned money and you don't make an effort or worst have no intention of paying back your loan, you will soon have "gaba" or "bukol". Why doesn't anybody make a teaching of paying what you owe and thanking that person for the help he has given you. Instead of paying them we are used to cursing the person who helped us during our critical time. We believe that soon he will be held responsible to God for what he did to you—asking his hard earned money back. But what does the Bible say about it? In Kings 4:7; Then she came and told the man of God. And he said, "Go, sell the oil and pay your debt, and you and your sons can live on the rest."

Psalm 37:21 says: The wicked borrows and does not pay back, but the righteous is gracious and gives.

Most people who are in deep debt, keep on acquiring additional debt for they believe that God will curse those people who will ask for payment of what they have lent—that's a very naïve and irresponsible belief.

The question now is, are we teaching great humanitarian practices or we are just a culture that does not know the meaning of integrity? If making an interest on the business you make is against Christian teaching, then why did God use the parable of talent. What is the essence of doing hard work if it is against the law of the universe to reap a reward?

Part of our culture teaches that money is the root of all evil. Try looking around. Isn't it that having no money is the root of all evil? Ask the robbers, the kidnappers, the snatchers or the hold-uppers or even the corrupt government officials. You will find out that having no money or lack of money is the root of their evil acts.

In the same manner, look at the people who have accumulated a mountain of assets and then later on started their own charity foundations to share the blessings they received. How many people have they been able to help to have a good education thru their scholarship programs? How many families were they able to help during calamities? How many homes were they able to build for those who had no shelter?

Some of these charity foundations have even encouraged us to have an entrepreneurial spirit by helping small business entrepreneurs.

Money is not the root of all evil, in fact; money is nothing in a real sense for it is just an idea. Remember we've discussed that money is equal to value—your value. Your true money or your true value does not lie in your wallet. It cannot even be found in any bank that you have an account with. It is found in your inner self. If you truly understand that, you can actually make or print any amount of money you desire; by just manifesting your true self . . . your true value.

It is the love of money, the love of earthly things which is the root of all evil. The attachment to its physical form and selling your true self and value in return for the money makes anybody evil. If you don't know how to use the value of money, then accumulating it is just like chasing the wind, just like what the bible says.

Indeed if you want to learn the basics of financial planning one good book to read to enhance your knowledge of money management is the Bible.

Gen. 41:47 say: "During the seven years of abundance the land produced plentifully." Isn't that true that even today, our life is like a cycle that there is a period of abundance and a period of famine? So what does the Lord ask us to do during the period of abundance?

Gen. 41:34-36: "Let Pharaoh appoint commissioners over the land to take a fifth of the harvest of Egypt during the seven years of abundance. They should collect all the food of these good years that are coming and store up the grain under the authority of Pharaoh, to be kept in the cities for food. This food should be held in reserve for the country, to be used during the seven years of famine that will come upon Egypt, so that the country may not be ruined by the famine."

If we have just learned a lesson from the bible that we are to keep a part of what you make during the period of abundance then sure enough, you will not be a slave of loan sharks and other lending institutions, just like what happened to the people of Israel. They did not keep or save during abundance period so they ended up selling their freedom to the Pharaoh (Gen. 47:13, 18-21 Joseph and the Famine]. It's the same thing with us, if you don't know how to keep a part of what you've earned, then you will sell your freedom in return for a safe and secure job.

Remember financial security does not mean financial freedom. If you go back to the history of the Philippine's freedom from her conquerors, it did not come from the desire of having security. It came from the courage of taking risks and the courage of standing on our own. If our great national heroes taught security then maybe up to now we would still be under the power of other mighty subjugators. Just like what happened to the Israelites, they sold their freedom for food security in order for them to survive during famine, and the consequence was that it was not only they who suffered. They passed it on to their great-grand children. And that is what's happening to most of us. We always cling to financial security for the fear of taking risks in exchange of freedom. In effect, we pass our slavery to our children and to the children of our children. We will be working all our waking lives.

The Bible teaches us to be wise even in how we budget and spend our hard earned money: Proverbs 10: 4-5 say: "He who has a slack hand becomes poor, but the hand of the diligent makes rich. He who gathers in summer is a wise son; he who sleeps in harvest is a son who causes shame."

The Bible also teaches us on how to grow our money: Ecclesiastes 11:2 "Divide your portion to seven, or even to eight, for you do not know what misfortune may occur on the earth."

That's how good the Lord is as a financial planner for even He teaches the importance of diversification. The Bible even mentions the importance of having the right mentor: Proverbs15:22 "Without consultation, plans are frustrated, but with many counselors they succeed."

So now, if you think that God does not want you to be rich then think again, for you may be missing out on your true purpose driven life. We have to accept that for us to do our mission, money plays a big part in it. Money is not everything but just a mere tool to fulfill our life's mission in this temporary world. Imagine how many people you can help if you are a rich missionary. Even the mere state of being rich for selfish reasons will mean a lot; you will no longer be one of the people needing to compete for benefits of government or private charity.

I can almost hear you say "But the Bible says that it would be much easier for the camel to enter in the eye of a needle than for the rich man to enter the gate of heaven." That parable is the main reason why we are afraid of becoming financially successful. For most of the religious leaders taught us a wrong doctrine on money.

In my long spiritual life that I have here on earth, one thing I'm just sure of; the God I knew is a generous and abundant God.

Yes I do believe in that parable—if money becomes the main factor or center of your life; if you detach yourself from your Creator and think that you and God are separate, if you see yourself with what you have, what you've accomplished, how big your house is, how big your bank account is, how high the position you held in your company is, then definitely it would be much easier for the camel to enter the narrow gate than a person who has a tight grip to the material world.

CHAPTER 6

DRAWING A PASSAGE PLAN
FOR YOUR SUCCESS

"Man is not the creature of circumstances;
circumstances are the creatures of man.
We are free agents, and man is more powerful than matter."
Benjamin Disraeli

It was a chilly early afternoon. Winter was approaching and a crisp November wind was blowing as I leaned on the side railings of our ship, enjoying the green scenery that was passing by. We were approaching the Cape Cod Canal on the way to Rhode Island, Massachusetts. It was my first visit to the land of the free called America on board an oil tanker which carried crude oil that we loaded at Yanbu, Saudi Arabia.

I enjoyed watching the birds flying all around, while some were diving in the water to catch fish. We were navigating inside the channel of the river guided by colored buoys on both sides. In navigation, buoys are one of the more important navigational aids. As with lighthouses, they guide ships into the right path of the channels and sometimes it even tells you if you are headed into danger. They direct ships into deeper parts of the water that is safe to pass through.

Inside the channel you have to stay in between the two buoys. If you veer away from that, you will be heading into the shallower parts of the water and you'll soon find yourself headed towards wreckage. Buoys are positioned at regular intervals that as soon as you pass a pair, another pair appears. While the previous one is disappearing on your stern, a new pair is emerging in front of you. They help you to continue on your journey that even if you are not familiar with the place, you will arrive in your destination safely.

Same in life, our goals serve as our buoys. Every time we accomplish one, we must have another one until we reach our desired destination. Like channel buoys, whenever we start deviating from our goals [buoys] we will be heading into disaster. Life without goals is like sailing a boat without a rudder. It steers our direction, that even if you have the best boat engine or the toughest sails, if your rudder is not functioning, your boat will end up where you won't want it to go.

The picture in the previous page is one of the ships I have previously sailed with. It is a chemical ship that carries industrial chemicals, sometimes alcohol and vegetable oils. I took that picture by climbing on a forward mast one sunny day when I noticed that the re-painting job of our deck was almost completed.

As a Chief Mate of the ship, it is my job to make sure that our ship is maintained regularly on all aspects, whether on its operational ability and even in its cosmetic appearance. And every time I join a ship, I always make it a point that before I leave, it is in better shape and condition than it was before.

I always show that picture in my Financial Planning seminars that I give to my fellow shipmates or even to non-sea-goers. To which they laugh for they always say, "What is the relevance of that ship with financial planning?"

It is sad that most seamen work on board ships just for the money and not learn anything from it. Running a ship is just like running your own company. Everybody should do their assigned task for the vessel to operate effectively. In fact, my realization about financial planning surfaced when I first join the vessel to work as a cadet. Many crewmen fail to realize that the reason a shipping company earns millions of dollars every year is because of the efficiency and hard work of the crew running the vessel. I always tell them: "You are the reason why this shipping company is so rich and becoming richer everyday!"

But then why is it that when it comes to their personal or family management, they fail to make themselves rich like what they do for the ship owners?

When you are on board ship and sailing in the middle of the ocean you will see nothing but water all around you. You will not even know from where you have been and where you are heading by just merely looking at the sea. Then how come one ship navigates from one place to another without being lost in the middle of the vast ocean? How does one ship that sails from New York reach Singapore which is on the other side of the world? Most amazing of all is that they know when they will be arriving in Singapore even before they leave New York.

It is because the captain and the officers of the ship employ the art of passage planning.

Passage planning is the art of the preparation of navigation before embarking on any voyage. Prior to departure from port, the navigating officer will prepare a detailed passage plan from the pier where their ship is moored up to the next pier where they want to go. Regardless if this pier is in the same country they are in or in the other part of the world, the important point is, knowing your destination against your point of origin.

This is one of the most basic things that I have learned while working on board ship: that whatever you want in life, wherever you want to go, you can safely and effectively reach it as long as you have carefully planned it. There is absolutely nothing in this world that you cannot be, or do, or have, as long as you have planned for it and have taken the necessary actions based on your plan. You must also have the courage to correct your plan along the way if it is necessary.

In our academy, they define navigation as the art of conducting a vessel from one point to another in the safest and shortest possible route. That is the guiding principle of passage plan preparation—to arrive in a place in the shortest and safest possible route. Again, it's the same thing with life, we live it to the fullest by conducting our life from one point to another in the safest and shortest possible way so that we can attain our life's greatest desires.

For example if you want to be rich, you can do it by selling drugs or being a gambling lord. That is the shortest way but the question is—is it safe? Or you can be rich also by saving a part of what you earn in your piggy bank. It's safe indeed, for you don't harm anybody by doing that, but the question is—is it the shortest?

Sailors have been able to explore all the great seas. Man was able to fly in which was once just a fantasy. Engineers are now able to build the tallest buildings in the world. Man was able to walk in space and later on, in the moon. At one point in history, all these things were just mere fantasy which only a few people believed was possible. In general, man became successful in these areas of life by first having a well designed plan. This well designed plan is what we usually call our GOAL.

PRINCIPLE OF PASSAGE PLANNING

> *"Planning is bringing the future into the present so that you can do something about it now."*
> **Alan Lakein**

In planning and achieving safe passage, a ship's passage plan is divided into four distinct stages; Appraisal, Planning, Execution and Monitoring, in chronological order. In our personal life, we can employ these same steps to develop and achieve our goals.

STAGE 1: APPRAISAL

Before any voyage commences, the captain, together with his officers carefully study the proposed voyage thru the help of related navigational publications and information appropriate for the voyage. It includes gathering weather reports to see how the weather is in the area where the ship will be passing. Constraints or obstructions along the way are taken into consideration to make sure that they don't miss anything. They use an appropriate checklist developed through previous experiences to make the passage safe and effective.

This practice is also true in life if you want to achieve your goals. You have to appraise yourself as to what your current condition is against the destination you want to reach. You have to be true to yourself and be mature enough to accept what help you would need, whatever missing factor you think might be necessary in order to achieve your goal. This stage is the right time to acquire it or learn it.

You can do that by attending seminars, reading books and looking for the right people to seek for advice—a mentor, a person knowledgeable in his chosen field who you think can give you sound advice. Again, the most important investment that you must have is investment for your personal development. Never begrudge the money you spend for your personal development because that is your most important investment.

STAGE 2: PLANNING

After gathering information, the ship's officers will start making the plan. This plan consists of many details. It includes, but is not limited to, the planned track which shows what course or direction the ship should take. Determining the distance from the ship's original position to it's final destination will show them what speed to take in order for the ship to arrive at the destination at a desired date and time. Since all plans don't work out sometime, they also plan for abort/cancellation points for critical maneuvers, a Wheel over position, which is an appropriate time and location where you should alter your course for the next planned course.

It looks so technical for non-seafarers to do that plan, but in life it only means writing down the things you want and the steps needed to get what you want. After appraising yourself, by now you must have a clearer view of what you really want. Everything should be clearer by now. But that cannot happen by trusting in your memory alone. It is much effective if you have a written plan on how to accomplish your goal.

Your goal must state what mission you want to accomplish, your purpose why you want to have that. Remember if the Why is strong enough for the How, it would be easy. You must also know the approximate time when you'd want to accomplish it, so you can measure your progress. Like in a ship's passage planning, keeping a regular position of the ship is very vital because by doing so, you will know if you need to increase or reduce your speed depending on your desired ETA [Estimated Time of Arrival].

In a ship passage planning, they have an abort/cancellation point; so you too, must also have a contingency plan. How about if our plans don't work out? Does it make us losers? No, the moment you accept being a loser, you lose the voyage. It is then and only then you become a loser. Remember it's not how you end the race but it's how you finish the race. If things don't work out as you want, you must be mature enough to learn what went wrong and find the courage to rise up above that challenge.

Looking back, you'll remember that you had a lot of dreams in the past that did not materialize. The main reason being that most of us perceived that it was unachievable. Why? Because most of us believe only in tangible things. Dreams that are only in your mind will become difficult to achieve if we can't touch it. But the moment you write it down then it becomes tangible—you can now touch it and actually see/read it. What more if you make a well designed plan? Remember, any goal unwritten will remain only as dreams.

STAGE 3 EXECUTION

Having finalized the passage plan, and as soon as the ETA can be determined with reasonable accuracy, the voyage can now be executed; in accordance with the plan made by the ship's officers. The Execution stage is a combination of the first, second and third stage. In this stage, the ship's officer will still continue to appraise the situation, make adjustments in planning if necessary, while continuing its execution.

In life, this is the most critical stage. Most of us are very good when it comes to drawing a plan of what we want, but when it comes to action or execution we often fail or delay things. Highly successful people are biased towards action. This is the reason why majority of us, at one point in our lives, get a very creative idea, but just because we failed to act on it, we wake up one day and find that somebody is doing it already. It is now a lost opportunity, because you failed to take action on your dream.

If you think you have prepared well, then there is nothing for you to worry about. Even if the ocean of life looks very uncertain now, even if you encounter many typhoons, life goes on. It's time to let go of your mooring lines and start heading out to sea to reach your wildest dream.

The moment you commence your life's voyage, one thing is sure—that one day you will arrive. But where? At your desired destination or to a wreckage? Five or ten years from now, what vision can you see about yourself, will you be wearing the clothes you want to wear, driving the car you want to drive, living in a house you dream to live in, or eating the food you want to eat? Well planned passages will make the big difference.

STAGE 4 MONITORING

On board the ship, the passage plan should always be available at the navigational bridge. This is to allow the duty officer immediate access to the details of the plan made. In fact before taking a watch, the first thing that the relieving officer will do is to refer to the plan to know the ship's progress in reference to it. It's the same thing with our goals.

The reason why we have to write it is for us to be reminded of what it was in the first place. Sometimes, in writing our goals, we become so excited only to find out that after a few days or weeks we've forgotten the written commitment we made to ourselves.

Almost all motivational speakers and authors recommend that we read our goal every day. Some say it's better if it is the first thing we see in the morning and the last thing we hold before we go to sleep at night. With this, whenever we feel upset, we can be reminded that temporary disappointments doesn't mean defeat.

The moment you start to make your goal, break it down into smaller stages, and complete each and every stage. This will definitely make you feel successful and it will surely elevate your self-esteem. In life, you will never be a winner unless you set a clear benchmark for yourself where you can measure your success. Success is very personal and relative; your personal achievement may be a failure for others and others' achievements may not be desirable to you. That's why it is important that you define your own personal goal in life. If you don't do it, nobody will.

But make sure your goal is not all about money; maybe one of your goals is to accumulate money as much as you can. But life is not meant to be lived for money alone. Construct goals for your personal development, career, love and relationship, community and spiritual well being. Only then can you experience total well being, or as others call it: the real wealth of life.

CONTINUOUS VOYAGE PROGRAM

Once you become a goal oriented person, you will learn that success comes from the way you deal with life. You learn that success is not a destination but a journey and that in every step along the way that you fight well to win your daily battles is already success that you can claim.

Arriving at your set destination doesn't mean that you are successful now. Yes, maybe at the moment but the question is— will it remain a success forever? Success is not having what you want. You must remember that success is how you did it rather than what you get from it. Success is passing all the hardships and challenges you have endured, rising up above the people that sought to bring you down. But you will never appreciate it by what you get. But if you are that kind of person, then surely, even if you get what you want, your heart will remain empty.

But let's say you indeed savored the process, the voyage that you have taken, for you to be successful. Will your success end there? The answer is no!

Let us go back to our analogy on how we do it on board the ship. Upon departure from New York, the captain and the rest of the crew have already carefully planned their voyage to Singapore. They addressed all the pertinent questions—what speed to use, how much fuel to take, where to pass (via the Suez Canal or the Cape of Good Hope in Africa] and what publications and maps needed to be on board before the vessel departs. Lets say that particular vessel becomes successful on their voyage and arrived safely and in a short time in Singapore. Will that be the last voyage of that vessel just because it already performed a successful voyage? Of course not!

I've worked on a particular tanker (a ship that carries oil products and chemicals] and that ship happened to land a hiring contract called a time charter, from one of the biggest major oil companies in the U.S, the Exxon Mobil. Our trading area was in the U.S. Gulf, the Caribbean and some parts of South America. I could say that the vessel was very successful at that time because after it was chartered by Exxon, we receive four voyage orders at a time. We were still working with one voyage when the company gave us another voyage even if we're not done with the first one yet.

This was very much unlike what happened in one of my previous ships, also a tanker. After twenty six years of its faithful service, our good captain received an order from the company to bring the vessel to India and intentionally run the vessel aground in the area where ships are scrapped. That was its final voyage. Yes, after twenty six years of producing millions of dollar, the vessel was finally decommissioned by its owner. Would you call that final stage of her service a success? Would being run aground in one of the beaches in India and being chopped up by the scrappers be considered a success?

It's the same thing in life. Not because you've accomplished one thing, does it mean you should stop there. Unfortunately for most people, that is what they do. We were raised with the idea that having numerous desires is evil. We were taught by some of our religion teachers that for you to be able to enter the kingdom of God you should eliminate desires in your life. I don't know with you, but the God I know is not selfish and narrow minded.

Success is measured on what trails you will leave this world when you are gone. I know that having a goal and working on it is a tedious job let alone having a numerous goals. But that's how you will appreciate life—the challenges that you have taken.

A real winner is the one who knows how to differentiate challenges and defeats. Once you give up your dream whenever life gives you a challenge, then and only then do you become defeated. Winners acknowledge that challenges are temporary disappointments and that it's a normal part of life, and a true winner rises above these challenges and learn from it. They continue on their journey towards their most awaited rewards— the realization of their dreams.

Having clear goals and mustering all your efforts in achieving them will surely increase your power and charisma. People around you will perceive you as a disciplined and determined person. Then you will notice that the world around you will move aside to give way to a person like you who knows where exactly he wants to go and what exactly he wants to do. It will make you a better person and you will be admired by people around you. And everything will fall into places. You will attract the right people and the right opportunities because the universe will make sure that you will have what you want to have. The world around you will conspire to give what exactly you have attracted into your life. Some call this the "Law of Positive Attraction" As what the law says, "There is nothing that you cannot be, do, or have."

MY LAST THOUGHTS

"I've come to embrace the notion that I haven't done enough in my life. I've come to confirm that one's title, even a title like President of the United States, says very little about how well one's life has been led. No matter how much you've done or how successful you've been, there's always more to do, always more to learn, and always more to achieve."

Barack Obama,
Arizona State
Commencement Speech,
2009

Making mistakes in life is not a major reason of life's failure but not learning the lesson from it is. That is also true with our financial challenges.

There was a couple named Aling Flor and Mang Tony. Aling Flor was a hard working mother but was not able to get ahead with her finances. Not because she was a bad person, but because she just failed to manage her finances and didn't even bother planning for the future. Our financial success is not based on how good or bad a person we are, but how effective our plan is. Financial blessings are not biased to what kind of person we are but on how we see the value of money.

Aling Flor and her husband Mang Tony raised their children very well, they were living in abundance when all their children were still young. But the moment their children started studying in college, everything changed drastically. They began to experience great financial scarcity.

Every time their money gets tough, the couple always tell their children that the reason they are experiencing financial difficulty is because of them, that they were the reason why they had to work hard.

Many parents use that mantra. We tend to make our children as the excuse as to why we are facing our current financial challenges; where in fact, if we had just made a plan ahead of time and took full control of our financial goals, we will not suffer that adversity.

What was the reason why they were having difficulties in sending their children to school? Did Aling Flor and Mang Tony just find themselves waking up one morning and that their children are already 16 years old and life surprised them with the realities that they have to send them to college? No, sending them to college is not a surprise; rather it is an obligation of all parents to provide for their offspring. And not to prepare for it until they are 16 years old is very naïve!

But if you ask most parents to make a list of reasons why they are experiencing a hard time; a lot of them are going to include in their list everything and every person except themselves. Then they wonder why in the world their children do not perform well in their education despite all their efforts in sending them to a good school.

Think about it, if your children will always hear that the reason why you are in great difficulty was because of them, what do you think their opinion will be about education? Do you think they will be inspired to study or they will despise it? For sure they will perceive it as useless and burdensome. I don't think your children will be inspired to perform well in school knowing that every day they stay at school is also a day their parents have to suffer.

So instead of blaming your children for your financial disaster; be reasonable enough to accept the reason why you are in disarray and start cleaning up your mess. Never get out of that predicament without getting something—that something is the great lesson it will give you. Above all, be humble enough to teach that same lesson to your children, so that they will not suffer the same predicament in the future.

I always watch the fights of Manny Pacqiao when I'm on board the vessel. The ship's crew had also never lost interest in it for we always watch it repeatedly on DVD. One of the highlights of the fights is not the fight itself but who will sing the Philippine national anthem. As a music lover and partly nationalistic, I always feel poignant whenever the singer renders the song in whatever way they deliver it.

For me, the fact that you hear your national anthem sang on international T.V. is more than enough to be proud as a Filipino. But most Filipino critics in our country don't share the same feelings with me. I remember the fight where Martin Nievera sang the national anthem, which for me it was so soulful indeed. But back in the Philippines, it raised a lot of criticisms. Some said that it was ridiculous, un-nationalistic and unconstitutional and guess what; everybody suddenly became a master of the Philippine constitution which nobody usually pays interest in. It caused a heated discussions everywhere for more than a week. The same thing happened when Arnel Pineda did the rendition.

But what does the constitution actually say about it? R.A. 8491 says that Lupang Hinirang "shall be in accordance with the musical arrangement and composition of Julian Felipe."

I've tried to research what caused this heated debate about the original composition of Julian Felipe. And you know what I found out? That the national anthem should only be performed by a pianist or by a brass band, as these were the only versions that were produced by Julian Felipe. That the Philippine national anthem was first written in the Spanish language, though R.A. 8491 also states that Lupang Hinirang "shall always be sung in the national language." Furthermore, because of its original time signature of 2/4 as compare to its present quadruple time of 4/4, it will be much difficult for us to sing it for it was designed to be a march song for our brave Katipuneros.

Meaning to say, all of us were committing a grave constitutional offense. Funny though that I'm now sounding like a constitutional lawyer like many others attempt to do.

Even in our political arena, whenever we have a present leader most of us become big critics. But political emotions aside, all of our past presidents had done something that we can be proud of, each one of them made a good thing though not a perfect service for the county. But look what is happening now; every time people rally on the street they shouted for one thing "IBAGSAK ang administrayon ni . . . !"

Then when a new leader is elected, a lot of people reminisce on the past leader and hailing them just to ruin or reject the present leadership. We can only praise the past but we hardly live in the present. I'm still hoping that one day we can muster all our courage to rally on the street and shout "ITAAS!" instead of "IBAGSAK!"

Why am I saying this? My point is that we are the creators of our own world. Whatever is happening in our personal lives, whether it is good or bad, we are the one who created it. Therefore, there is no one to blame but ourselves if circumstances are against us, or to give credit to ourselves too when things are going right.

One time when I told my friends that I was going to write a book about financial planning and the subject was on how to become rich and successful, they became hesitant at first. Maybe they were thinking on what authority I can write on that subject if I myself am not as rich as Henry Sy, Manny Villar, Gokongwei or other rich and famous personalities in our society.

Again as I said in the beginning, being rich and being poor is relative. The main problem why we are poor or why we don't have enough or why we are not good enough is because we always compare ourselves with an outside barometer. We keep on competing with our siblings, relatives, neighbors or friends. One moment we want a particular thing or possession but the moment we have it and see that people around us have newer things with them, instead of being happy and appreciative on what we have accomplished, we start to blame again our self for not having the things that other people have.

So what is the secret of becoming happy and appreciative with your accomplishments? Never compare yourself with other people around you but compare yourself to what you were before. Maybe my friends were right that I may not be as rich and famous as other people I have mentioned, but now I could say that I'm rich and famous, compare to whom?—to my old self and becoming more and more wealthy and successful every day.

Whenever I conduct a seminar I always use the quote of Lao Tzu from his teaching The Tao Cheng. He said "There is no way to happiness, because happiness is the way". Five or ten years from now, even if you acquire your most desired goal but if you don't know the purpose why you want to have it in the first place, for sure you will still be unhappy.

Looking back on my life's condition if I may compare the life I have now, I can really say that I've gone far . . . . farther than I could have ever imagined. Maybe nobody really knows what life tomorrow will bring to us. But now one thing I am really sure of, is that even if I go back to my previous life's misery, or even worse than it was before, one thing I am sure now is, I can regain whatever I might lose—for now I know how to feel good about life, whatever it may look like. And that's the real secret of life, feeling good for everything it gives.

For me, that is the greatest inheritance I could ever give to my children—to see life in a positive way!

And THAT requires no estate tax.

Whatever you are doing right now, no matter how diminutive it is in the eyes of people around you, as long as it makes you happy and gives you good reason to wake up in the morning, do it and continue on doing it. Do not be surprised if one day someone will ask you how you became so successful. If you can't find happiness with your life's achievement then maybe that's not success after all, because success means happiness. And true enough there is no way to happiness because happiness is the way—THE WAY TO LIFE'S SUCCESS.

If you understand this, then you can reclaim yourself and be free from the everyday problems of life—yes you can gain even financial freedom. And with that it would be easy for you as it is easy for me to say "YES I AM RICH!"

"Rich and successful compared to whom" they may ask, compare to when I was twenty, fifteen, ten, five years ago or even compare to what I was yesterday. Indeed being rich and poor is relative. If you change the way you look at things, then the things you look at will change.

You'll surely continue to face challenges, life's difficulties and disappointments. You have to accept that they are an unavoidable and inevitable part of human development and experience. But if you will just learn to gather together your available resources, continue to develop it and to respond effectively, sure enough you will grow and become a better person. In fact, without those challenges that you've encountered, you will not be the kind of person you are today.

Take charge of your life and take charge of your finances today.

After all money is not about a number it's about mindset.

"The purpose of life is to matter, to count, to stand for something, to have it make some difference that we lived at all."
Leo Rosten, *b. 1908,*
American writer

Say good words,
have good thoughts,
do good deeds, and
help make a world of difference.

Master Shih Cheng-Ye
Still Thoughts

HELP YOUR LOVE ONES!

Now that you know the secret on how to get rich, it is your responsibility to share it to your love ones. If you don't, you've got a big problem! Without sharing what you have learned on how to improve life and achieve your dreams—your loved ones could still be your great liability.

What can you do to help them? Teach them what you've learned. Time is running out for them. They need your help—now. Maybe you are the angel that they've been asking God to send them.

If you really think they have to change their negative mindset into positive, don't wait for somebody else to help them. Be the first person whom they can count on. Make a big difference in their lives so that they will remember you and even by their great-great grand children. For you have uplifted their life situation that benefited their whole family.

You have now invested in your future. Why not invest a little amount for them too. Give them a copy of this book today—"Financial Planning for the Fast Changing World—How to Grow Your Money While Making Yourself Grow at the Same Rate You Ever Dream Possible.

I have done my share for this mission, now it's your turn to do yours!

Christopher G. Cervantes

RECOMMENDED READING

RICH DAD POOR DAD by Robert T. Kiyosaki with Sharon L. Lechter

CASHFLOW QUADRANT by Robert T. Kiyosaki with Sharon L. Lechter

THY WILL BE DONE by Atty Angelo M. Cabrera

THE POWER OF NOW by Eckhart Tolle

FILL YOUR LIFE WITH MIRACLES by Bo Sanchez

MY MADE INVEST IN THE STOCK MARKET by Bo Sanchez

THE RICHEST MAN IN BABYLON by George S. Clason

GO NEGOSYO, 50 INSPIRING ENTREPRENEURIAL STORIES by Joey Conception

UNLIMITED POWER by Anthony Robbins

THINK AND GROW RICH by Napoleon Hill

THE SUCCESS PRINCIPL by Jack Canfield

THE INTELLIGENT INVESTOR by Benjamin Graham

THE SNOWBALL, WARREN BUFFET

AND THE BUSINESS OF LIFE by Alice Schroeder

THE SEVEN HABITS OF HIGHLY EFFECTIVE PEOPLE by Stephen R. Covey

THE MILLIONAIRE NEXT DOOR: THE SURPRISING SECRETS OF AMERICAN'S WEALTHY by William D. Danko

NOTES

NOTES

NOTES

NOTES

NOTES

NOTES

NOTES